My First

STUDY BIBLE

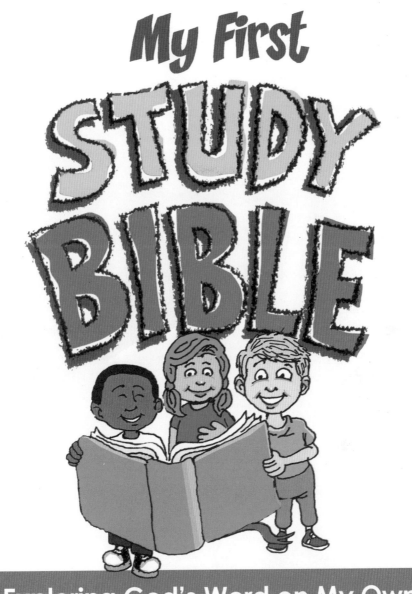

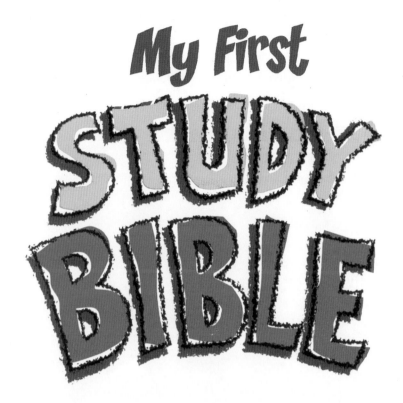

My First STUDY BIBLE

Exploring God's Word on My Own!

Paul J. Loth

Illustrated by Rob Suggs

THOMAS NELSON
Since 1798

For other products and live events,
visit us at: **thomasnelson.com**

Table of Contents

OLD TESTAMENT

NEW TESTAMENT

Welcome to My First Study Bible

The Bible is made up of 66 individual books. We call the Bible God's Word because God told the writers of the Bible what to say.

Introductions to the Books of the Bible
My First Study Bible introduces every book of the Bible. You will learn about all the writers, what books they wrote, and why they wrote them.

Help in Understanding the Bible
My First Study Bible also helps you understand the Bible better. Look for what is written in the special boxes. There you will find more information to help you understand each Bible story.

In *My First Study Bible* you will meet the Bible writers and Bible heroes.

May *My First Study Bible* help you better understand God's Word on your own.

Paul J. Loth, Ed. D.
Carol Stream, Illinois

OLD
TESTAMENT

LAW

I am Moses. God helped me write the first five books in the Bible: Genesis, Exodus, Leviticus, Numbers, and Deuteronomy. Some people call these books the Pentateuch. Others call them the Books of Moses or the Books of the Law. I wrote these books so people would know what happens when we obey God, and what happens when we do not obey Him.

Pentateuch refers to the first five books of the Bible.

GENESIS

The Book of Beginnings

I am Moses. Genesis is the first book I wrote. I wanted everyone to know how the world began. I also wanted everyone to know about the people who lived a long time ago. We can learn a lot from them.

God Gave Us a Beautiful Home

Genesis 2:18—3:24

I'm Adam, the first person God made. After God made me, He let me live in a very beautiful garden.

Everywhere I looked I saw trees, plants, and water. When I wanted something to eat, I just took some fruit from one of the trees. The garden was full of animals and birds. God even let me name them.

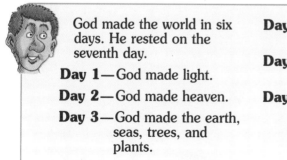

God made the world in six days. He rested on the seventh day.

Day 1—God made light.

Day 2—God made heaven.

Day 3—God made the earth, seas, trees, and plants.

Day 4—God made the sun, moon, and stars.

Day 5—God made the birds and fish.

Day 6—God made the animals and Adam!

He also made Eve, the first woman.

As much as I liked the garden and animals, God knew that I needed someone like me. He made a wife for me. Her name was Eve.

God told us we could eat anything in the garden except the fruit from one special tree. "If you eat from that tree, you will die." Eve and I didn't want to die.

The tree from which they could not eat was called the tree of the knowledge of good and evil. God told Adam and Eve they would die if they ate from that tree.

One day a cunning serpent started talking to Eve. "Did God tell you not to eat from these trees?"

"We can eat anything we want," Eve explained, "but we can't eat from the tree of the knowledge of good and evil or we will die."

"You won't die," the serpent assured her. "You will be like God."

Eve believed him. She took a bite of fruit, and I did, too.

The serpent was really Satan. He was trying to make Adam and Eve disobey God, and he still tries to make people disobey God. Satan never quits!

Then we heard God walking through the garden.
We ran away to hide.

"Where are you?" God called.

Eve and I knew we should say something. We didn't want
to be in more trouble than we were already in. "I heard You
coming," I told God, trying to think fast, "so I hid because . . .
I am naked."

"Did you eat from the tree?" God asked me.

He knew! We couldn't hide what we did any longer. I blamed my wife: "Eve gave me the fruit to eat!"

"Why did you do that?"

God asked Eve.

"The serpent lied to me," Eve told God.

God made us leave the beautiful garden, and He punished the serpent, too. We had disobeyed God.

Think About This

God means what He says. God told Adam and Eve they could eat anything they wanted except one thing. But Adam and Eve thought God didn't really mean what He said. So they ate the forbidden fruit! But God punished Adam and Eve because they did not obey Him.

God Kept Me Safe

Genesis 6:11—7:18

Hi! I'm Noah. I loved God very much. My family and I lived at a time when everyone disobeyed God and made Him sad.

One day God spoke to me. He was very angry. "People have filled this world with too much violence. I will destroy everyone and everything. Make yourself an ark because I am bringing a flood."

I worked hard on that ark. It was big!

 An ark is a big boat. It was 1½ football fields long, 2 football fields wide, and 5 stories high!

God told me, "Bring your family into the ark. I will save you because you obey Me. Also bring male and female animals of every kind." Once we were all inside, God shut the door. Then it rained and rained and rained.

We spent over a month in the ark before we heard the rain stop. Then one day I let a dove loose. When it came back, I knew it had not found any dry land. Seven days later I let the dove out again, and this time it came back with a leaf in its mouth. The next time I let it go it did not come back at all. The earth was dry now, and God told us we could leave the ark.

The first thing we did on dry ground was to worship God.

God also brought water out of the earth and the seas. Water was everywhere!

Then God made a beautiful rainbow. He told us, "This rainbow is a reminder to you. Never again will a flood destroy the world. That is My promise."

Think About This

Have you ever seen a rainbow? Sometimes you can see one after it rains. A rainbow is a reminder of God's promise. God said He will never flood the whole earth again.

God Kept His Promises

Genesis 21:1–7; 22:1–19

Hello, my name used to be Abram, but God changed my name to Abraham. My name means "father of many nations." That's what God made me.

27

I married Sarai. Then God told us to move to a new home He made for us. When Sarai was an old woman, God changed her name to Sarah. He told me she would have a son.

Abraham grew up in Haran but then he moved to Canaan. It was a long trip, but he was glad he obeyed God and moved. Later God gave the land of Canaan to Abraham's great-grandchildren. Moses led them there.

I laughed. My wife and I were very old. It was not even possible for us to have children anymore. It didn't make sense. But I believed God.

Sarah and Abraham were in their nineties! In fact, Abraham was seventy-five years old when they moved to their new home. He didn't expect to take care of a new baby when he was one hundred!

God kept His promise, and Sarah did have a child. We named him Isaac. Then something very strange happened. "Take Isaac," God told me, "and sacrifice him to Me." I didn't understand, but I obeyed because I loved God.

Isaac and I traveled to the top of the mountain. I prepared the fire and the wood for the sacrifice. Then I lifted my hand to kill my only son. God stopped me. Now He knew I would even give up my only son for Him. Many years later, God sacrificed His only Son, Jesus, to save us from our sins.

One reason God asked Abraham to sacrifice Isaac was so everyone would think about what it meant for Him to send Jesus to die for our sins.

When Isaac grew
up, he had two sons
of his own, Jacob and
Esau. Jacob's children
became the nation of
Israel. They were
God's chosen people.

My grandchildren became many nations. That was what God promised. God always keeps His promises.

Our Family

Abraham had another son, Ishmael. Both Isaac's children and Ishmael's children became strong nations. Isaac's descendants through his son Jacob became God's chosen people, the nation of Israel.

Think About This

Do you think that some things just can't happen? Abraham and Sarah thought so. They thought they were too old to have a baby. But God can make the impossible happen! God gave them a little boy.

God Makes Good from Bad

Genesis 37:14–28; 42:1—45:5

I am Joseph. I was one of Jacob's twelve sons. A long time ago something terrible happened to me, but God took care of me.

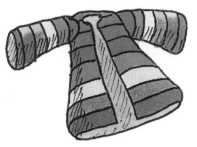

My dad liked me better than any of my brothers. He even made me a beautiful coat. That made my brothers very angry.

One day my dad said to me, "Go check on your brothers. I want to be sure they are all right." They were taking care of the sheep near another city.

Joseph's brothers called him "the dreamer." God gave him a special ability to understand dreams. One of his dreams was that his brothers would bow down to him someday. Joseph's brothers did not like that, but his dream was right.

"Here comes that dreamer," they said. "Let us take care of him!" They grabbed me and tore off my coat of many colors. Then they threw me into an empty pit.

Then traders going to Egypt came by. One of my brothers said, "Instead of killing Joseph, let us sell him to these men as a slave." That is what they did.

Many years later my family had no food to eat because their land had become very dry. My dad said to my brothers, "Go to Egypt and see if you can find some food there."

A slave was someone who was owned by another person. A slave worked and was not paid. People paid for slaves and sold them to other people.

So my brothers traveled to Egypt. They came to the king's palace to ask a certain man about the food. I was that man but my brothers did not recognize me! God had helped me while I lived in Egypt. I started out as a slave, but I had become a very important person in the nation.

One day, after my brothers had traveled to Egypt a second time, I told them who I was. "I am Joseph, your brother." They were so surprised they couldn't talk. Then I told them, "Do not be sad or angry because you sold me as a slave. God sent me here to Egypt to save your lives." They had wanted to hurt me, but God had a special job planned for me.

Think About This

Joseph's brothers sold him into slavery. God was in control of all that happened. He kept Joseph safe so he could help his brothers later on. God always has a reason for what He does.

EXODUS

The Beginning of a Nation

I am Moses. Exodus is the second book I wrote. It talks about what happened when I led the people of Israel out of Egypt. The book of Exodus is the story of what I saw God do. It tells about God saving the people of Israel from slavery. It tells how He helped us cross the Red Sea. It tells how God gave me the Ten Commandments.

The book of Exodus contains my life story. I was there!

God Keeps My Baby Brother Safe

Exodus 2:1–10

I am Miriam. Do you have a little brother? I did. Let me tell you how God saved his life.

Our family was living in Egypt. Pharaoh, the king of Egypt, was not nice to us. He made slaves of all the Hebrew people and made us work very, very hard. Then he decided that our families were growing too fast. He said that all boy babies had to die.

Some of the people called Miriam and her family the Hebrews. That is because they were all related to Abraham, the first Hebrew.

When my baby brother was born, my mom hid him for three months. She did not want him to die. One day my mom could not hide my brother any longer. She made a basket that would float. Then she put my baby brother in the basket and put it at the edge of the Nile River.

Miriam had an older brother, too. His name was Aaron. He would be an important helper to Moses when they grew up.

Miriam's mom made the basket by weaving together tall plants that grew near the river. Then she covered the outside of it with sticky tar. That kept the basket—and her brother—from sinking.

The Nile River was a big river in Egypt. Many people went swimming, took baths, and even washed their clothes in the river.

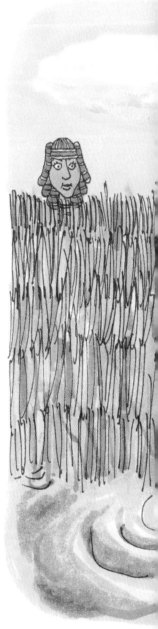

I stood beside the river—far enough away
that people wouldn't know I was watching
the basket. Then I heard voices. I looked
down the river and saw a group of women in
the water. One was the daughter of Pharaoh,
the king of Egypt!

She sent one of the women to get the basket for her. She opened the basket, and my brother started to cry.

Pharaoh's daughter acted as if she felt sorry for my little brother. She said, "This is one of the Hebrew babies." She didn't seem to want him to die either.

I went to where the women were standing. "Do you want me to call one of the Hebrew mothers to take care of the baby for you?"

Pharaoh's daughter said just one word to me. "Go!" I ran to get my mom.

"Please take care of this baby for me," Pharaoh's daughter said to my mom. So my mom had her baby back.

Many of Miriam's relatives helped deliver and take care of the babies when they were born. Pharaoh's daughter didn't know Miriam was getting the baby's own mother!

When my brother was older, he went to live with Pharaoh's daughter. She named him Moses. My baby brother grew up in the palace of the king of Egypt.

God kept my baby brother safe. He had a special plan for him. When Moses was older, he helped our nation. God really took care of us.

Moses wrote the Books of the Law, the first five books in the Bible. He also led his people out of slavery in Egypt to the Promised Land.

Think About This

Do you have a baby brother or sister? Do you help your parents care for the baby? Miriam did. She had a baby brother named Moses. God used Miriam to help keep baby Moses safe. God helps our families keep us safe.

God Teaches Pharaoh a Lesson

Exodus 2:11–15, 21; 7:14—12:31

Who are the most important people you know? Do they think they can do anything they want?

I had to convince Pharaoh, the king of Egypt, that he should obey God. It was not easy. I am Moses and I would like to tell you about it.

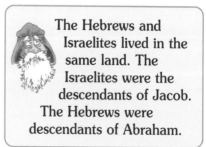

The Hebrews and Israelites lived in the same land. The Israelites were the descendants of Jacob. The Hebrews were descendants of Abraham.

I am an Israelite, but I was raised in the palace of the king of Egypt. One day I saw an Egyptian being mean to an Israelite. I killed the Egyptian. Then I was afraid I would get in trouble, so I ran for my life.

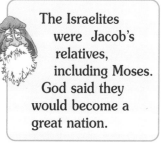

The Israelites were Jacob's relatives, including Moses. God said they would become a great nation.

I ran to a place called Midian. I married a woman there named Zipporah. One day, I saw fire coming out of a bush, but the bush was not burning up. I stopped to look at it.

"Moses, Moses!" a voice called to me from the bush.

"Here I am," I said.

"Take your sandals off, for the place where you stand is holy ground."

It was God! He told me to return to Egypt. He wanted me to help the people of Israel get out of Egypt and escape from the mean king.

My brother, Aaron, and I went to Egypt to talk to Pharaoh. "God has a message for you, Pharaoh," we told him. "God says, 'Let my people go.'"

Pharaoh did not listen. In fact, he made the Israelites work harder. I was really upset.

Moses told God that he did not speak very well. So God told him he could tell Aaron what to say and Aaron could speak for him.

Egypt was the most important nation on earth. Pharaoh was the king of Egypt. He did not think he had to listen to Moses. He did not even think he had to obey God!

God told me to talk to Pharaoh again. I was not surprised when Pharaoh said no again. So Aaron threw his rod on the ground. It turned into a snake, just as God had promised me it would. Pharaoh just laughed. His magicians threw their rods on the ground. They became snakes, too. But God's snake ate all their snakes. Even though God proved He was the most powerful one, Pharaoh still said no.

The next morning Pharaoh was walking to the great Nile River. Aaron and I met him and said, "God says 'Let my people go!' To prove that God has sent us, all the water in the land will be turned to blood." Then Aaron lifted his rod out over the Nile River and God changed all the water into blood. Pharaoh still did not obey God.

Moses was a shepherd when he first talked to God. He used a wooden stick to help him take care of the sheep. It was called a rod. God used Aaron's rod to make Pharaoh obey Him.

The battle was not between Pharaoh and me. The battle was between Pharaoh and God. It continued. God brought frogs into the land of Egypt. Frogs were everywhere!

Pharaoh still did not obey the Lord. Then the lice came. Pharaoh did not listen, so the Lord sent flies.

Pharaoh and his friends in Egypt believed in a lot of gods. But God is stronger than any of them. Everything God did defeated one of the Egyptian gods. He showed Pharaoh that He is the only true God.

One of the plagues God sent to the Egyptians was lice. Lice are small insects that sting.

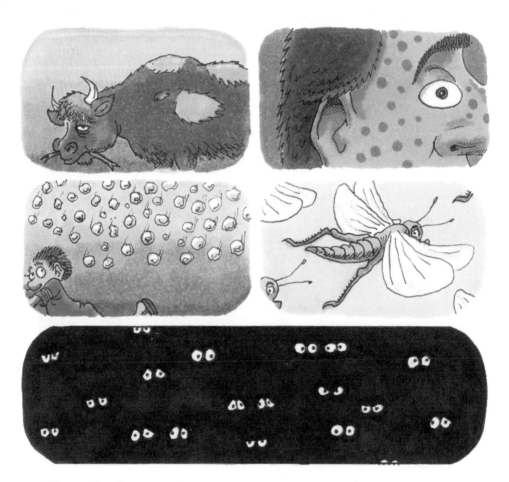

Then God sent a disease that killed the Egyptian cattle, horses, donkeys, camels, oxen, and sheep. Pharaoh still did not obey God. Next God caused the Egyptians to have boils (big blisters). Then God sent a hailstorm. Then locusts invaded the land of Egypt. Finally, God sent darkness. It stayed dark for three days!

Nothing made Pharaoh listen.

Then God said the oldest child, the oldest slave, and the oldest of each kind of animal in every Egyptian family would die.

When that happened, Pharaoh told me the Israelites could leave. Finally! After being slaves for over 400 years, the Israelites were free.

That night we had a special meal together. It was called the Passover Meal. God asked us to have a Passover celebration every year so we would remember how He brought us out of Egypt.

God asked us to kill a lamb and spread the lamb's blood over our door so that He would not kill our oldest children or animals. He would pass over our houses.

God Saves My Friends

Exodus 14:1–28

Pharaoh, the king of Egypt, finally let me and the Israelites leave Egypt. Then he changed his mind. Keep reading and I, Moses, will tell you more.

Pharaoh didn't want to lose us. He liked having us there to do all his work. I thought Pharaoh had learned to obey God. But he was very stubborn. He sent the army of Egypt after us.

We marched and marched until God told us to camp near the Red Sea. Then we heard the army coming! The sea was in front of us, and the Egyptian army was behind us. We were trapped.

The Red Sea was a big sea. Because Moses and the Israelites didn't have any boats, they thought they were trapped in the middle of the wilderness. It was pretty scary!

Everyone was scared and started yelling at me! "It would have been better for us to serve the Egyptians than that we should die in the wilderness."

"Do not be afraid," I called out to them. "Stand still, and see the salvation of the Lord. The Lord will fight for you, and you shall hold your peace."

I held out my hand over the Red Sea, and the water started to move. Soon we could see the bottom of the sea. We walked right across. But the Egyptian army followed us.

Then God told me to stretch out my hand again. I did, and the Red Sea went back to the way it was before. Water rushed over every animal and every person in the Egyptian army. We were safe!

After the Israelites saw how carefully God had protected them, they believed His promises. They believed me, too.

The Egyptian army used chariots, wagons that were open in the back and could hold three men. Each chariot had two wheels and was pulled by horses. The soldiers fought mostly with bows and arrows and spears.

Think About This

God said the Israelites should be free. But things looked hopeless for them. The Red Sea was in front of them and the army was behind them. God parted the water so the Israelites could walk right through the Red Sea. Nothing is hopeless when God is involved.

LEVITICUS

God's Handbook for Living

Leviticus is the third book God helped me, Moses, write. When we were in Egypt, we obeyed the rules of Egypt. Then God took us out of Egypt. He gave us new rules to follow. I wrote Leviticus so the Israelites would know God's rules.

God told me to climb to the top of a large mountain, Mount Sinai. I spent a lot of time with God there. God told me what He wanted the people of Israel to do. I wrote God's words in the book of Leviticus.

My Sons Disobeyed God

Leviticus 10:1–7

I am Aaron, Moses' brother. I helped Moses lead the people of Israel out of Egypt. My sons and I were priests of God. We helped the people worship God. I learned that God expected us to obey Him, just as everyone else should.

My sons, Nadab and Abihu, helped me serve the Lord. My sons thought they could do whatever they wanted because they were priests. But they were wrong.

One day Nadab and Abihu made a fire that God had not told them to prepare. So fire came out from the presence of the Lord, and my two sons died.

 A priest was someone who spoke to God for the people and helped them speak to God.

Moses said, "God told us that He should be regarded as holy and be glorified before all the people." God had told us how to worship Him. My sons knew what God wanted them to do. They did not think they had to follow God's rules.

If you met an important person, you would be very careful how you spoke to him or her, wouldn't you? God wants us to respect Him, too.

I did not even have a funeral for my sons. Moses was afraid God would punish me, too. I learned a big lesson. We must treat God with respect. I only wish my sons had learned that.

Think About This

God does not have special rules for special people. Aaron's sons did not respect God's power. If they had, they would have known His rules were for priests, too. God's rules are for everyone.

NUMBERS

The Book of Wanderings

I am Moses. Numbers is the story of how God helped me lead the people of Israel to our new home. It is a sad book. I led my friends to the land God had prepared for us. But they were too scared to go into the land. They were afraid of the people who lived there. So we had to   wander in the wilderness for another 40 years!

In this book you will read how I disobeyed God. Because I did not obey Him, God did not let me lead the people into their new land. My good friend and helper Joshua did that.

We Were Outv

Numbers 14:6–10

Have you ever had to make a decision with your friends? It is hard if some of your friends want to do one thing but some want to do something else. How do you decide?

I had that problem. Joshua and I wanted to do one thing. But ten of our relatives disagreed with us. My name is Caleb.

After Moses led us out of Egypt, he told us about the special place God had prepared for us, the Promised Land.

We were almost to Canaan when God told Moses to choose twelve men, one from each tribe of Israel. Moses asked us to go on ahead and report back about the land and the people.

 Moses tells about this on page 57. You might want to read his story.

Jacob was the grandson of Abraham. Jacob's name was changed to Israel. He had twelve sons. The children of his twelve sons became the twelve tribes of Israel.

The land was beautiful! We saw lots of fruit on all the trees. As soon as we got back, we told all the Israelites about the land. We even showed them the fruit we had brought back with us.

"Let us go up at once and take the land, for we are well able to do it," I told everyone.

Ten of the spies did not agree with me. "We are not able to go up against the people," they said, "for they are stronger than we . . . We saw the giants . . . and we were like grasshoppers."

Then everyone became scared. They even started to cry. "If only we had died in Egypt!" they complained.

Joshua and I spoke out. "The land we passed through is [a very] good land. If the LORD delights in us, then He will bring us into this land and give it to us . . . Only do not rebel against the LORD or fear the people of the land . . . The LORD is with us. Do not fear them."

71

The people of Israel did not believe us. In fact, they wanted to kill us. Worse, they did not want to believe in God. Even after all He had done for us. They wanted to go back to Egypt where we had been slaves. We ended up wandering in the

wilderness for forty more years because the people did not trust God. Joshua and I were the only ones who made it to the Promised Land.

Joshua became their leader. Later he led them into the Promised Land. They learned that no one can defeat God. Joshua tells about God knocking down the walls of Jericho on page 93.

Think About This

Do you trust in God? The two spies who trusted God were allowed to enter the land. The other ten spies died before God gave them the land. Not trusting in God can cause problems.

I Disobeyed God

Numbers 20:1–21

Hi! I am Moses. I loved God very much. I always tried to obey Him. God helped me lead the people of Israel out of Egypt and out of slavery.

Then God led us through the wilderness. Whenever there was a problem, God took care of it. But the people still complained. Sometimes they said they wanted to go back to Egypt. They complained about me and my brother, Aaron. They even complained about God.

Let me tell you about one of the times the people of Israel complained.

God led us out of slavery in Egypt through the wilderness to the Promised Land. The land was beautiful! But the people of Israel would not go into the land because they were afraid of the people who lived there. So we had to turn away.

The people of Israel had been slaves in Egypt for over 400 years. God freed them from Egypt, saved them from the Egyptian armies, and took care of them in the wilderness. You can hear more about it. Turn to page 57.

One day after we had been in the wilderness a long time, the people started complaining again. They had no water. "If only we had died when our friends died! Why have you brought us into the wilderness, that we should die here?"

Of course, God heard them.

"Take the rod," God told me. "Gather the assembly [people] together. Speak to the rock before their eyes, and it will yield its water."

I gathered everyone together. "Hear now, you rebels!" I said. "Must we bring water for you out of this rock?" Then I hit the rock twice with my rod and water gushed out.

This was a rod like the one Moses had used when God did all the wonderful things for them in Egypt. This time he used it to disobey Him.

God was not pleased. "Because you did not honor Me in the eyes of the children of Israel, you shall not bring them into the land which I have given them." I had disobeyed God.

 Moses tried to "show God up." He took things into his own hands and made everyone think he was doing everything for them. He struck the rock instead of speaking to it as God told him. God should be respected and obeyed. Moses did not do that.

Think About This

Have you ever lost your temper? Moses knew that he should do exactly what God told him to do. But he lost his temper and hit the rock instead of speaking to it. Because he disobeyed God, he was not allowed into the Promised Land. We should always do what God tells us.

DEUTERONOMY

Moses' Farewell

I am Moses. I led the people of Israel out of Egypt and gave them God's laws. I even asked God to save their lives. And I led them through another 40 years in the wilderness. God did let me see the special home He had prepared for us. It was beautiful!

Deuteronomy tells about when I said good-bye to my friends. That was just before I died. It is the fifth book I wrote. I wanted my friends to remember what God did for us. I wanted them to always trust in the Lord.

Moses Says Good-Bye

Deuteronomy 31—32

I am Moses. I once saw a bush burning in the desert and talked to God. It was hard to believe that God wanted me to lead the Israelites out of Egypt and into the Promised Land. But He did. God helped me each step of the way. Whenever there was a need, He met it.

When my job was over God told me that it was time for me to be with Him in heaven. I was 120 years old. Let me tell you about the last few days of my life.

When God told me I would die soon, I asked Him for one thing. I knew that the people of Israel would need a new leader. "Please set a man over these people so that they may not be like sheep which have no shepherd." God had already chosen Joshua to be the leader of Israel.

I finished writing my books. They were called the Books of the Law. I gave these books to the people of Israel. Then they would know what God wanted them to do.

 The Books of the Law are the first five books of the Bible. God helped Moses write them so everyone could learn about Him.

I said good-bye to my good friend, Joshua. "Be strong and of good courage," I told him. "And the LORD, He is the One who goes before you. He will not leave you nor forsake you."

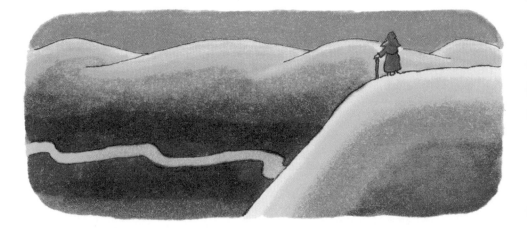

Then God told me to climb to the top of a high mountain. From there I could see the Promised Land that I would never live in. "Because you sinned against Me among the children of Israel at Kadesh, you shall see the land before you, though you shall not go there."

At Kadesh God told Moses to speak to the rock. Instead he hit the rock with his rod. To hear more about what happened, turn to page 74.

Think About This

One of the most important things Moses did was to write down God's teachings. We still read Moses' writings in the first five books of our Bible. They tell us what happens when we obey God and what happens when we do not obey Him.

HISTORY

Hi! We are Joshua, Samuel, Jeremiah, Ezra, and Nehemiah. We wrote most of the Books of History in the Old Testament. We want you to meet Ruth and Esther as well. Some people wrote Old Testament books about them, too. We are glad Ruth's and Esther's stories are part of the Books of History. The Books of History are Joshua, Judges, Ruth, 1 Samuel, 2 Samuel, 1 Kings, 2 Kings, 1 Chronicles, 2 Chronicles, Ezra, Nehemiah, and Esther. These books were written so everyone would know what happened to God's people.

These books have some happy stories and some sad stories. But all the stories show how God always took care of us. We were His children.

JOSHUA

Taking Over the Land

Hi! I'm Joshua. I was Moses' helper. After Moses died, I led the people of Israel into the new home God had prepared for us. You might know me as the person who led Israel around the city of Jericho.

This book is my story. I tell how God led me and the Israelites into our own home. God is so good! He took care of me and the Israelites and gave us a beautiful home in which to live.

I Chose God's Side

Joshua 2

Hi! My name is Rahab. I lived in a wall. It was a different kind of wall. The wall went around our city, Jericho. The wall was so wide you could walk on top of it. One day I made a big decision.

My neighbors in Jericho and I had heard about the Israelites. We knew God was on their side. We had heard how God freed them when they were slaves in Egypt. He even made a path for them through the Red Sea. We also knew that the Israelites had taken over the land on the other side of the Jordan River. We knew our city would be next.

The Jordan River was a big river near Rahab's home. The Israelites were already on the other side of the river. Rahab knew they would be crossing the Jordan River soon and heading for Jericho.

One day two men came to my house. They were Israelites, and they were planning to take over our city. The king found out about these men. He sent me a message. "Bring out the men who have come to you." I decided to hide those two Israelites even though that meant disobeying my king.

I sent the Israelites up to the roof. They hid under the stalks there.

The stalks were stalks of flax. These were three to four feet long. They were lying on the roof. It was easy to hide underneath them.

I told the messengers, "Yes, the men came to me, but I did not know where they were from. . . . When it was dark, they went out. I do not know where they went; pursue them quickly, for you may overtake them."

I went back up to the roof.

"I beg you," I pleaded with the two Israelites, "since I have shown you kindness, promise me that you also will show kindness to my family and save us from death."

"When the LORD has given us the land," the Israelite spies said to me, "we will deal kindly with you."

I let them down by a rope through my window. They would be safe now. I had chosen God's side.

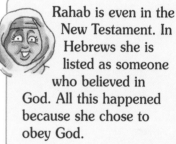

Rahab is even in the New Testament. In Hebrews she is listed as someone who believed in God. All this happened because she chose to obey God.

Think About This

Sometimes when people take a stand for God, it puts them in great danger. Rahab was willing to take that chance. She knew God was very powerful. She knew that she wanted to be on His side. We should always be on God's side.

God Knocked Down the Walls of Jericho

Joshua 6

Hi! I am Joshua. God helped me lead the people of Israel into the Promised Land. God was so good to us. I would like to tell you about one of our greatest victories.

We faced a very strong city after we crossed the Jordan River into the Promised Land. It was Jericho. There was a thick wall around it. The people of Jericho could hide inside the wall and be safe.

"I have given Jericho into your hand," God told me, "you shall march all around the city once. This you shall do six days. But the seventh day you shall march around the city seven times, and the priests shall blow the trumpets. When you hear the sound of the trumpet, all the people shall shout with a great shout; then the wall of the city will fall down flat."

Joshua and the Israelites had taken over the land on one side of the Jordan River. This was while Moses was their leader. Now it was time to cross the Jordan River. The first place they came to on the other side was the city of Jericho.

I explained the plan to the people and then we lined up. The armed soldiers went first. They were followed by the priests and the ark of God. We marched around the city once. Then we returned to our camp.

The next day we marched around the city of Jericho again. We did it again the next day, and the next day, and the next day, and the next day! For six days we marched around the city of Jericho.

The ark of God was important. The Israelites knew God was with them when the ark of God was leading them. The Ten Commandments were kept in the ark.

The seventh day came. We got up early—at dawn. Everyone found his place. We began to march as we had for six days. But this day was different. We marched around the city once, but instead of stopping after one time, we kept going. We marched around the wall seven times. As we were finishing our seventh lap around the city, the priests blew their trumpets.

I instructed the people:
"Shout, for the LORD has given
you the city!" Everyone shouted.
The priests blew their trumpets.
Then suddenly the wall of
Jericho fell down flat!

When we took over the city, we remembered Rahab. I turned to the two spies who had stayed at her home. "Go into her house," I told them, "and bring out Rahab and her family, just as you promised her." Then we entered the city. God gave us the great city because we obeyed Him.

Rahab kept two of the spies safe when they came to look at the city. They promised to keep Rahab and her family safe. To read Rahab's story, turn to page 87.

Think About This

When the people of Jericho saw Joshua's army marching around the city, they probably wondered why. They found out on the seventh day when the wall of the city fell down and Joshua's army came in. God has many ways to show His power.

JUDGES

The Result of Disobedience

I am Samuel. I was the last of the judges in Israel. Judges were important people in our nation then. We told the people what God wanted them to do. I was the judge who chose Saul and David to be kings of Israel. One of the judges many people remember was Samson.

The book of Judges explains what happened to our nation. We did not have a king then. Judges were our leaders. Of course, the real leader of our nation was God. He always took care of us.

God Speaks to Me

Judges 6

Did you ever want to be sure God was speaking to you? I did. My name is Gideon. I would like to tell you about my experience.

We had been having trouble in our land. Some people, the Midianites, were destroying our land.

One day God spoke to me. "I will be with you," He said. "Go in this might of yours, and you shall save Israel from the hand of the Midianites."

"But how can I save Israel? I am the youngest in my father's house."

God spoke again. "Surely I will be with you."

The Israelites' home, the land God gave them, had been taken over by the Midianites. God wanted them to have it back. He wanted Gideon to lead the Israelites to reclaim it.

102

I had to be sure God was speaking to me.

"I shall put a fleece of wool outside," I said. "Tomorrow if there is dew on the fleece only, and it is dry on all the ground, then I shall know that You will save Israel by my hand, as You have said."

A fleece is a piece of wool.

So that is what I did. I woke up early the next day. The fleece was dripping wet. The dew from the fleece filled up an entire bowl!

"Do not be angry with me," I said to God. "Let me test just once more with the fleece; let it now be dry only on the fleece, but on all the ground let there be dew."

The next day the fleece was dry. But the ground was wet. God was with me!

I Learned to Trust God

Judges 16

My name is
Samson. I was a
very strong man.
This is my story.

Before I was born the Angel of the LORD came to my mother and told her she would have a son. The angel said I would be a Nazirite and that I would save Israel from the Philistines.

The Philistines were my enemies. They had been hurting the people of Israel for over 40 years. Now they were trying to hurt me because they had heard how strong I was.

A Nazirite was someone who made a promise to serve God. Samson was not supposed to drink wine, cut his hair, or touch a dead body.

The Philistines said that they would give Delilah a lot of money if she helped them.

One day I met a woman named Delilah. I liked to be with her. Some Philistine rulers found out and came to visit Delilah.

"[Trick] him, and find out where his great strength lies, and by what means we may overpower him."

So the next time I saw Delilah, she said to me, "Please tell me where your great strength lies, and with what you may be bound."

"If they bind [tie] me with seven fresh bowstrings," I told Delilah, "then I shall become weak."

So Delilah tied me up. Then she yelled, "The Philistines are upon you, Samson!" But I just snapped the strings. I had not told her the real secret of my strength.

Delilah wouldn't give up. "Look," she said, "you have mocked me and told me lies. Now please tell me what you may be bound with."

I answered her, "If they bind me securely with new ropes that have never been used, then I shall become weak."

She tied me up again, this time with new ropes. Then she shouted, "The Philistines are upon you, Samson!" I just broke the ropes again as if they were pieces of thread.

Delilah tried to get my secret out of me one more time. "Until now you have mocked me and told me lies. Tell me what you may be bound with."

"If you weave the seven locks of my hair into the web of the loom," I told her, "then my strength will be gone."

Delilah did exactly what I told her. Then she woke me up shouting, "The Philistines are upon you, Samson!" I simply pulled apart the fabric on the loom and I was fine.

Samson had promised never to cut his hair. So his hair was very long. He told Delilah to weave seven locks of his hair into the fabric she was making on her loom and then hold it with a pin.

Then Delilah said to me, "How can you say, 'I love you,' when your heart is not with me? You have mocked me these three times, and have not told me where your great strength lies."

Day after day Delilah kept pestering me. I became very annoyed. So I finally told her the truth. "No razor has ever come upon my head," I told her. "If I am shaven, then my strength will leave me, and I shall become weak."

Then one day when I was taking a nap at her house, she had a man shave my head. The next thing I knew Delilah was shouting, "The Philistines are upon you, Samson!" I tried to escape, but I did not realize that God had left me. My strength was gone. I became a slave of the Philistines. But soon my hair started growing back!

One day the Philistines were all together worshiping their god. It was not the true God, but their make-believe god. They brought me out in front of them so they could make fun of me. I put my hands on two pillars of the building.

I prayed to God. "O LORD God, strengthen me just this once that I may with one blow get revenge on the Philistines."

I pushed the pillars as hard as I could. God gave me the power to knock down the pillars. The whole building crashed to the ground, killing me and everyone in it. I defeated more of my enemies by dying than I had during my entire life.

Even though he disobeyed, God still used Samson to destroy many Philistines, the enemy of the people of Israel.

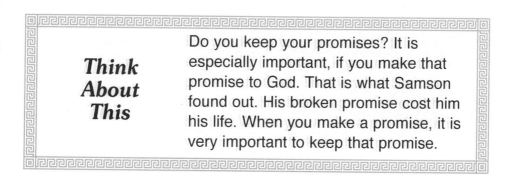

Think About This

Do you keep your promises? It is especially important, if you make that promise to God. That is what Samson found out. His broken promise cost him his life. When you make a promise, it is very important to keep that promise.

RUTH

The Reward of Faithfulness

I am Ruth. My great-grandson was King David. Many years later an even greater king, Jesus, was born to our family.

Some sad things happened to me, but God gave me a happy ending because I trusted in Him and obeyed Him. I am glad someone wrote my story in the Bible. I want everyone to know how good God was to me.

I Followed God

Ruth 1—4

My name is Ruth. My husband and I lived with his mother, Naomi, in the land of Moab. My father-in-law, Elimelech, had already died. My husband and his brother were Naomi's only living relatives.

Then one day my husband died. His brother died, too. My mother-in-law, Naomi, my sister-in-law, Orpah, and I were left alone.

Naomi, my mother-in-law, decided to go back to her old home in Judah. She told Orpah and me to return to our parents.

Orpah and I cried. "We will return with you to your people."

"Turn back, my daughters," Naomi said. "Why will you go with me?"

Ruth grew up in Moab. Her home was just a little south of Judah. Her father-in-law had moved his family to Moab before he died. That is how Ruth met her husband.

Naomi thought Ruth and Orpah wanted her to have more sons so they could marry them. But that wasn't why they wanted to stay with her. She was their family now. They did not want to leave her alone.

Orpah and I both cried again. Then Orpah left. "Look," Naomi told me, "your sister-in-law has gone back to her people; . . . return after your sister-in-law."

"Urge me not to leave you, or to turn back from following after you," I begged her, "for wherever you go, I will go; and wherever you stay, I will stay; your people shall be my people, and your God, my God." Naomi knew I was determined to go with her. So she finally let me go with her.

When we arrived at Naomi's home in Judah, her friends and relatives were excited to see her. Naomi told them she had come home empty.

Naomi felt empty because her husband and two sons died. She felt God was punishing her. But God had another reason. He would still take care of them.

She had a relative, Boaz, who was very rich. He let me pick grain in his field. He was very kind to me, helping me find food and giving me water to drink.

"Why have I found favor in your eyes?" I asked.

"It has been fully reported to me, all that you have done for your mother-in-law since the death of your husband," Boaz explained to me. "A full reward will be given you by the LORD God, under whose wings you have come for refuge [protection]."

Boaz and I were soon married. We had a son, Obed. Obed's son, Jesse, became the father of David, king of Israel. Imagine that! My great-grandson became the king of Israel.

1 SAMUEL

Qualities of Good Leaders

I am Samuel. I was a gift from God. My mother was Hannah. She asked God to give her a baby. He did—me. I grew up with Eli, the priest.

I became a leader of the people. First Samuel tells my story. It is really a history book. It tells what happened to my nation, Israel.

121

My Prayer Was Answered

1 Samuel 1

Have you ever wanted something a lot? Did you pray about it? I did. In fact, I wanted something so much that I offered to give God something back in return, if He would answer my prayer. Have you ever said that to God?

My name is Hannah. I would like to tell you how God answered my prayer.

My husband loved me very much. But I did not have any children. I was miserable. "Why do you cry?" my husband asked me. "Am I not better to you than ten sons?"

Other people thought there was something wrong with Hannah because she did not have any children. They laughed at her because they thought they were better than her.

I was so upset I cried and could not even eat. My husband and I went to worship God. I asked God to give me children. "O LORD," I prayed, "if You will give me a baby boy, then I will give him to the LORD all the days of his life."

The priest, Eli, saw me. I told him how sad I was and how hard I was praying. "Go in peace," Eli told me, "God grant you what you have asked of Him." I felt much better then. I even ate again.

Eli was the priest. His job was to help people obey God. Eli would also give them messages from God.

God remembered my prayer, and we had a son! I named him Samuel.

Samuel was special. As she promised, Hannah took Samuel to stay with Eli in the temple so he could serve God. Hannah's son became a leader of the people of Israel for a long time.

Think About This

Have you ever prayed to God for something you wanted? Hannah did. She wanted a baby very much. She knew that only God could help her. God answered her prayers by giving her Samuel. God will answer our prayers, too.

I Heard Voices in the Night

1 Samuel 3

Do you ever hear a voice calling you at night? I did. The voice I heard was God. I am Samuel. Let me explain.

My mother was Hannah. She had asked God for a baby, and I was God's answer. Mom promised God that she would give me back to Him to serve Him. So when I was still very young, Mom took me to the temple to stay with Eli, the priest. I helped Eli in the temple.

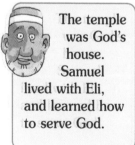

The temple was God's house. Samuel lived with Eli, and learned how to serve God.

128

One night I heard a voice calling me.

I ran to Eli, "Here I am."

"I did not call you," Eli said, "lie down again."

I went back to lie down. Then I heard the voice again: "Samuel!"

I ran back to Eli.

"Here I am," I told him.

"I did not call you," Eli said, "lie down again."

I lay down again, but then I heard the voice a third time!

I got up a third time. "Here I am," I told Eli. "I know you called me."

For the third time Eli told me to lie down again. But he also told me something else. "If you hear the voice again say, 'Speak LORD, for Your servant hears.'" Eli had decided that someone really was calling me and that someone was God.

I went back to bed. Then the LORD came into my room and called me again: "Samuel! Samuel!"

This time I didn't run to Eli. I answered the way Eli had told me, "Speak, for Your servant hears!"

Eli was right. I was hearing the voice of God. God had a special message for me. He told me what He wanted me to do. And He told me what He was going to do in Israel because people had disobeyed Him. God spoke to me many times in my life. God became my special friend.

God had some special things to tell Samuel. He wanted him to help the people of Israel learn to obey God.

Think About This

When your mom or dad calls you, do you answer right away? Samuel answered right away when he heard someone calling him. It was God who called Samuel. He had some special things to tell Samuel. We should always listen for God's call.

God Chose His Own Man

1 Samuel 16:1–13

Have you ever tried to read someone's mind? Could you do it? I am Samuel. I was God's prophet in the Old Testament. Let me tell you about when I tried to read God's mind.

"I have rejected Saul from [ruling] over Israel," God told me. "I am sending you to Jesse. I have provided Myself a king among his sons."

So I went to visit Jesse. He lived in Bethlehem. I invited Jesse and his sons to come with me to sacrifice to God.

Bethlehem became known as the "City of David." Jesus was born in Bethlehem.

They would give an animal as an offering to God. That is how they told God they loved Him. It was called a sacrifice.

Jesse was the grandson of Ruth and Boaz. Turn to page 114. Ruth will tell you why she was special to God.

I saw Jesse's son, Eliab. "Surely, this is the one God has chosen to be king."

But I was wrong. God reminded me: "Do not look at his appearance, because I have refused him. For the LORD does not see as man sees; for man looks at the outward appearance, but the LORD looks at the heart."

I looked at another son of Jesse, Abinadab. "Neither has the LORD chosen this one," I said to Jesse. Then I saw Shammah, Jesse's next son. But he was not the one either. I saw seven of Jesse's sons. They walked in front of me one by one. God did not choose any of them. But God had told me that one of Jesse's sons would be the next king. "Are all the young men here?" I asked Jesse.

Jesse said, "The youngest one is keeping the sheep."

"Bring him," I said. "We will not sit down until he comes here."

When David left his sheep and came to see me, God said, "Arise, anoint him, for this is the one!"

I took a horn of oil and anointed David as the next king. When God looked at David, He did not see a young boy. He saw the great leader David would become.

 Anointing a person's head with oil was a special way of treating royal people. Jesus was anointed with oil, too, when He was on earth. Samuel's action showed everyone that David was chosen by God.

Think About This

People should not be judged based upon age or looks. When Samuel looked for the new king he found that out. God looks at the heart and knows if a person will serve Him. It does not matter how the person looks on the outside.

I Was a Giant Killer

1 Samuel 17

My name is David. I was one of the kings of Israel. God took good care of me. I would like to tell you about one of the first times God took care of me. I was a young person, not much older than some of you.

I had many older brothers. Three of my brothers were in the army for the nation of Israel. One day my dad said to me, "Take these ten loaves, and see how your brothers are, and bring back news of them."

When I arrived at the battle I ran to find my brothers. Then I heard about Goliath. "I defy [go against] the armies of Israel this day," Goliath had said, "give me a man that we may fight together."

Goliath was really big! He was over 9 feet tall! That is almost as high as the basket used in a basketball game.

All the men of
Israel started to run away
when they saw this huge man.
"Have you seen this man who has
come up?" the soldiers asked me.
"Surely he has come up to defy Israel."

I was not afraid. "Who is this Philistine, that he should
defy the armies of the living God?" I asked some men around
me. I asked other soldiers the same question. When King Saul
heard what I was saying, he asked to see me.

I explained my thoughts to him. "Let no man's heart fail because of Goliath. I will go and fight with this Philistine."

"You are not able to go against this Philistine to fight with him," the king said to me, "for you are but a young boy."

"I have killed both lion and bear; and this Philistine will be like one of them, seeing he has defied the armies of the living God. The LORD will deliver me from the hand of this Philistine."

"Go," King Saul told me, "and the LORD be with you."

The king put his armor on me, a bronze helmet and a coat of metal. I tried to walk around. "I cannot walk with these," I said, taking off the armor. I was not used to armor. I picked up my staff and took my sling with me.

David's staff was a long stick. He used it when he walked and when he took care of his sheep. He used his sling to protect his sheep. A sling was usually made of several long pieces of rope or leather attached to a piece of leather that held a stone. David also had a pouch to keep stones in.

I stopped at the brook, picked out five smooth stones, and put them in my pouch. Then I began to walk toward Goliath. He walked toward me. He saw how young I was, and he started making fun of me: "Am I a dog that you come to me with sticks?" he yelled. "Come to me, and I will give your flesh to the birds of the air and the beasts of the field!"

"You come to me with a sword, with a spear, and with a javelin," I yelled back to the giant. "But I come to you in the name of the LORD of hosts! . . . This day the LORD will deliver you into my hands; . . . for the battle is the LORD's!"

I ran toward Goliath. I reached into my pouch and pulled out one of the five stones. Then I slung the stone toward Goliath. It hit him right in the forehead. He fell down on his face.

All the soldiers in the Israelite army shouted and ran after the Philistines. God had won the battle. He had given Goliath into our hands.

Think About This

Do you think someone who is young could do something wonderful for God? David was just a young boy and he won a battle for the whole Israelite army. Everyone can serve God!

2 SAMUEL

The Story of King David

I am Samuel. I was God's prophet in the Old Testament. God helped me choose David to be king of Israel. He was a special king. King David loved God very much. He tried to obey Him. Second Samuel is the story of King David. It tells about the good things David did.

It also tells what happened to our nation when Saul and David were the kings. At first 1 Samuel and 2 Samuel were one long book. Now you can read each book separately.

I Want to Worship God

2 Samuel 6:1-19

Do you go to church? Why? What do you do there? Do you worship God?

I am King David. I loved God very much, so I made a special place for God. I would like to tell you about it.

Jerusalem was our capital. It was also my home. I wanted it to be God's home, too.

I found a special place for the ark of God in Jerusalem. I even made a tabernacle (tent) to cover it.

The ark of God was where God's Spirit lived in the Old Testament times. Now God's Spirit can live in your heart.

152

Then I called the priests and the Levites. "Sanctify yourselves," I told them, "that you may bring up the ark of the LORD God of Israel to the place I have prepared for it."

Moses divided the nation of Israel into twelve tribes. They were named after the twelve sons of Jacob. The Levites were the special tribe of priests. They helped us worship God.

There was a special way to carry the ark of God. No one could touch the ark. Only the Levites could carry it. And they had to carry it a special way.

The ark of God was holy. God wanted to be sure they treated it that way. The Levites slipped two poles through rings attached to the side of the ark. (There were two rings on each side.) Then they lifted the poles onto their shoulders.

So the Levites talked to their relatives. Some of them were singers. Some of them played musical instruments. Some played harps and cymbals.

Everyone in Israel gathered to take the ark of God to Jerusalem. As we walked, we sang music to God. We shouted and we blew trumpets. We praised God for being so great!

We placed the ark of God inside the tabernacle at the special place. Then we told God how much we loved Him. "Give thanks to the LORD," I urged the people of Israel. "Sing to Him! Talk of all His wondrous works!"

Before we went home I blessed all the people. Then I gave everyone a loaf of bread and piece of meat and raisin cake.

Think About This

Some Christians do not have churches to gather in for worship. In some countries the Christians must meet secretly. Have you thanked God for your church and the freedom to worship together with other Christians?

1 KINGS

The Divided Kingdom

Hi! I am Jeremiah. I was a prophet of God. I told people to obey God. Many times they did not like what I told them. Sometimes I had no friends and even my family became angry at me. That made me sad. It is hard not to have any friends.

This book is about a sad time in our nation. We were a strong nation for a while when Solomon was king. But then our nation divided into two countries. Many of the people did not love God anymore. I was very sad. God was sad, too.

I Wanted to Be Wise

1 Kings 3:1–15

What do you say when people ask you what you want for a present? What would you say if God asked you what He should give you? I had that choice. I am King Solomon. I loved God very much.

My father was King David. He loved God very much. In fact, God called my dad a man after His own heart.

After I became king, God said to me, "Ask! What shall I give you?"

Solomon's father was not perfect, but he loved God. He tried to please God. That is why God loved him so much.

I answered that incredible question. "You have shown great kindness to Your servant David, my father," I said. "Now, O LORD my God, You have made me king instead of my father David, . . . give me an understanding heart to judge Your people, that I may discern [know the difference] between good and evil. For who is able to judge this great people of Yours?"

Israel had become a very large and powerful nation. Solomon knew that he would need God's wisdom to be a good king.

God was happy. I could have asked for a long life or riches, but I did not. God was glad I asked for wisdom. He told me, "Because you have asked this thing . . . I have given you a wise and understanding heart, so that there has not been anyone like you before you, nor shall any like you arise after you. And I

have also given you what you have not asked: both riches and honor, so that there shall not be anyone like you among the kings all your days. So if you walk in My ways . . . as your father David walked, then I will lengthen your days."

God kept His promise. People came from all over the world to hear my wisdom and to see my riches.

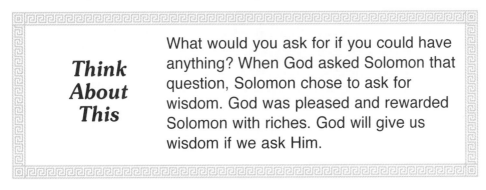

Think About This

What would you ask for if you could have anything? When God asked Solomon that question, Solomon chose to ask for wisdom. God was pleased and rewarded Solomon with riches. God will give us wisdom if we ask Him.

I Solved the Mother's Problem

1 Kings 3:16–28

When two of your friends have an argument, how do you decide who is right?

I am King Solomon, and I would like to tell you about a decision I had to make. Two mothers came to me one day. They had a problem. "This woman and I live in the same house," one of the mothers said. "This woman's son died in the night. So she got up in the middle of the night while I slept and took my son from my side, and laid him next to her and laid her dead child next to me. And when I got up in the morning, there was my son— dead. But when I looked at him, he was not my son."

Solomon's wisdom was from God. People from all over the world came to ask his advice.

"No!" the other mother said. "The living one is my son, and the dead one is your son!"

The first woman yelled back at her, "No! The dead one is your son, and the living one is my son!"

I said to them both, "The one says, 'This is my son, who lives, and your son is the dead one'; and the other says, 'No! Your son is the dead one, and my son is the living one.'"

"Bring me a sword," I said.

I continued my directions. "Divide the living child in two, and give half to one, and half to the other."

 Solomon was not really going to cut the baby in half! He knew the real mother would not want him to hurt her baby. The baby's real mother would be willing to give up her baby to save his life.

"O my lord," one of the mothers said, "give her the living child, and by no means kill him!"

The other mother said, "Let him be neither mine nor yours, but divide him!"

I knew then that the first woman was the baby's real mother. "Give the first woman the living child, and by no means kill him," I said. "She is his mother."

God's gift of wisdom helped me to know how to make the right decision.

Think About This

Have you ever tried to settle an argument between two friends? It is hard to know who is right. Solomon had to choose which woman was telling the truth. He was glad he had asked God for wisdom. Solomon made the right choice. We should always ask God to help us with difficult choices.

God Takes Care of Me

1 Kings 17:1–16

What happens when you disobey your parents or teachers? Are you punished? Ahab, king of Israel, disobeyed God more than any king before him. God punished Ahab for his evil ways. I had to deliver the bad news to Ahab. My name is Elijah. I was God's prophet in the Old Testament.

God told me to tell King Ahab that it was not going to rain again until I said it should. That was Ahab's punishment for leading the people away from God.

Elijah delivered God's message to the king. Then he waited for God to tell him when it should rain again.

After I spoke those words to Ahab, God told me, "Get away from here . . . and hide by the Brook Cherith, which flows into the Jordan. I have commanded the ravens to feed you there."

I did what God said. In the morning the ravens brought me bread and meat to eat, and I drank from the brook. Then in the evening the ravens brought me more food. God took good care of me. But one day the brook dried up. I had no more water to drink.

God took care of Elijah near the Brook Cherith. Then when He wanted him to move on, He took care of him in a different way.

"Get up," God told me, "go to Zarephath and stay there. I have commanded a widow there to provide for you."

When I got to Zarephath, I saw a widow picking up sticks. I called to her, "Please bring me a little water in a cup, that I may drink." The woman started off to get me some water. I called to her again, "Please bring me a morsel of bread in your hand."

"As the LORD your God lives," she explained to me, "I do not have bread, only a handful of flour in a bin, and a little oil in a jar."

It might seem that if Elijah took the woman's flour and oil, she would have nothing left. She and her son would starve. But she trusted God. She obeyed God and He took care of all of them.

"Make me a small cake from it and bring it to me," I told her, "and afterward make some for yourself and your son. For thus says the LORD God: 'The bin of flour shall not be used up, nor shall the jar of oil run dry until the day the LORD sends rain on the earth.'"

The woman did what I told her. After that, she always had enough flour and oil. It did not run out. God kept His promise. God also kept His promise to Ahab and kept the rain from coming for three years.

Think About This

Some people think their actions do not affect anyone else. That is not true. When God punished Ahab by stopping the rain, everyone in the land had trouble finding food. God made sure Elijah had food.

God Is Up to the Challenge

1 Kings 18:1–39

I am Elijah. I was God's prophet a long time ago. King Ahab and Queen Jezebel did not obey God. Many of the people in Israel did not obey God either.

One day I saw King Ahab. "Is that you, O troubler of Israel?" he said to me.

"I have not troubled Israel, but you have," I said to Ahab. "You have forsaken the commandments of the LORD. Now therefore, gather all Israel on Mount Carmel and the 450 prophets of Baal."

King Ahab and Elijah did not get along too well! The king did not obey God. He even tried to get other people to disobey God, too.

Baal was a make-believe god. Many people believed in him. Elijah wanted to prove that Baal was not real.

So King Ahab sent a message to the prophets of Baal. They met me on Mount Carmel. There were many people there.

"How long before you decide who to believe?" I asked the people. "If the LORD is God, follow Him; but if Baal, follow him."

No one said anything. I had a plan. We would make two sacrifices, one to God and one to Baal. But we would not light the fire under either sacrifice.

"You call on the name of your gods," I said, "and I will call on the name of the Lord; and the God who answers by fire, He is God."

Everyone agreed. "It is well spoken," they all said.

So the followers of Baal prepared a bull for sacrifice to Baal. Then they asked Baal to light the fire under the sacrifice. "O Baal, hear us!" they said. Then they started jumping up and down.

They called to Baal all morning.

"Cry aloud," I told them, "he is meditating, or he is busy, or he is on a journey, or perhaps he is sleeping and must be awakened."

So they cried louder.

All these prophets jumped up and down and screamed until evening. But there was no answer.

"Come near to me," I said to everyone. Then I made a sacrifice to the LORD. I built a trench around the altar. "Fill four waterpots with water," I told some of the people, "and pour it on the sacrifice and on the wood."

When they were done, I said to them, "Do it a second time." So they poured more water on the sacrifice and the wood underneath the sacrifice.

"Do it a third time," I said. They poured four more waterpots of water on the sacrifice. By this time the sacrifice was soaked. The trench around the sacrifice was filled with water, too.

"Hear me, O LORD, hear me," I prayed, "that this people may know that You are the LORD God!"

The sacrifice caught fire! The fire was so strong it even dried up the trench filled with water. All the people fell down on their faces. "The LORD, He is God! The LORD, He is God!" they shouted.

God proved Himself to the people of Israel. He is the only God.

Think About This

God sent fire crashing down from heaven to prove to the prophets of Baal that He is the true God. God is more powerful than anyone or anything.

2 KINGS

The Road to Captivity

My name is Jeremiah. I was a prophet of God in the Old Testament. I had a tough job. God told me to tell people that they were doing the wrong thing. Many people were not very happy with me. Second Kings was written so everyone would know what happens when we do not obey God. The book of 2 Kings explains how other countries took over our nation because we disobeyed the Lord.

At one time 1 and 2 Kings were one book. Now they are two separate books.

God Brought Me Home in Style

2 Kings 2:1–18

I am Elijah. I was a prophet of God in the Old Testament times. Many of the people did not obey God. I had to tell them that they were wrong. One day I even had to fight with the prophets of Baal. God helped me prove that the Lord was the only God.

God had told me that Elisha would be the prophet who would take my place. When I told Elisha that God had chosen him, he came with me everywhere I went.

Now it was time for me to go home to be with God. Elisha would continue helping people obey God. I was looking forward to going to heaven. I wanted to be with God.

Elisha and I were together in Gilgal. It was time to say good-bye. "Stay here, please," I told Elisha. "The LORD has sent me on to Bethel."

"I will not leave you!" Elisha told me. So Elisha and I went on to Bethel.

Elisha wanted to learn all he could from Elijah about serving God. Elijah was only going to be with him a short time. That's why Elisha would not leave him.

When we got to Bethel, the sons of the prophets there came to talk to Elisha. "Do you know that the LORD will take away Elijah from you today?" they asked Elisha.

"Yes, I know," Elisha said, "keep silent!"

"Elisha, stay here, please," I urged. "The LORD has sent me on to Jericho."

"I will not leave you!" Elisha insisted. So we went on to Jericho.

Some of the prophets were young men. God gave them messages for the people.

The same thing happened there. The sons of the prophets came to talk to Elisha.

"Do you know that the LORD will take Elijah away from you today?" they asked Elisha.

"Yes, I know," Elisha told them, "keep silent!"

I tried again. "Stay here, please," I told Elisha. "The LORD has sent me on to the Jordan."

"I will not leave you!" Elisha told me again. So we walked on toward the Jordan River.

When we got to the river, I took my mantle off. Then I rolled it up and hit the water with it. The water divided. Elisha and I walked across without getting wet.

A mantle is a cloak or coat that Elijah wore over his shoulders.

After we crossed the river I asked Elisha a question. "What may I do for you before I am taken away?"

"Please let a double portion of your spirit be upon me," Elisha asked me. That was asking a lot.

"You have asked a hard thing," I told Elisha. "Nevertheless, if you see me when I am taken from you, it shall be so."

God gave Elijah His Spirit to help him do the right thing. Elisha wanted God to help him, too.

We talked some more. Then suddenly a chariot of fire pulled by horses of fire landed right between us. I was going home to heaven! Soon I was taken up by a whirlwind into heaven.

And Elisha saw it all! As I was leaving, Elisha yelled, "My father! My father! The chariot of Israel and its horsemen!" Elisha would become a great prophet. God would take care of him. And I was going to heaven on a chariot of fire!

Think About This

The things God does are amazing. Taking Elijah to heaven in a chariot of fire was a reward for Elijah and a testimony of God's power.

I Helped a Widow

2 Kings 4:1–7

Do you like helping people? I do. My name is Elisha. I was a prophet of God in the Old Testament times. I began serving God by working with Elijah. He was one of God's prophets.

I would like to tell you about one of the first people I was able to help. She was a poor widow.

"Your servant my husband is dead," a woman cried to me one day. She was very upset.

"And you know that he loved the Lord. And the person to whom I owe money is coming to take my two sons to be his slaves."

The woman's husband was one of the sons of the prophets. He worked with them telling people to obey God. He loved God very much.

When people had no money, the person they owed took some of their family members to work for free. That is how people paid back debts.

"What shall I do for you?" I asked her. "Tell me, what do you have in the house?"

"I have nothing in the house but a jar of oil," she said.

"Go, borrow vessels from everywhere, from all your neighbors—empty vessels," I told her. "And when you have come in, you shall shut the door behind you and your sons; then pour the oil into all those vessels."

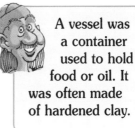

A vessel was a container used to hold food or oil. It was often made of hardened clay.

The woman did as I told her. Then she went back into her house and closed the door behind her. When she came out her door again, she told me the amazing thing that had happened inside.

She had taken
her one jar of oil
and poured it into
the first vessel. Her
son gave her the
next vessel, and she
poured more oil into
that. Then she filled
a third vessel.

She poured oil into all
the vessels she had.
When she had asked one
of her sons to bring her
another vessel, he said,
"There is not another
vessel." And there was no
more oil left.

 God would have
kept giving the
widow oil.
Whatever
number of vessels
she needed to fill,
God would have
taken care of her
needs.

After she told me her story, I told her, "Go, sell the oil and pay your debt; and you and your sons live on the rest."

Think About This

God helped Elisha perform a miracle to save the widow's sons from slavery. God cares about the problems His people have.

I Obeyed God

2 Kings 22

Would you like to be a king? I became king of Judah when I was eight years old. I am King Josiah. Would you like to know what it is like to be king? I would be glad to tell you.

The most important thing about being king is to try to do the right thing. I had heard of King David. So I tried to do what he would do. That made God happy.

King David was special. He was called a man after God's own heart. To read more about David, turn to page 151.

When I was 26 years old, we were repairing the house of the LORD. I sent Shaphan, the scribe, to the temple. "Go up to Hilkiah, the high priest," I told him, "that he may count the money which has been brought into the house of the LORD."

Shaphan helped Josiah a lot. A scribe was important. He helped write down God's words. The priest was important, too. He helped people worship God.

When Shaphan saw Hilkiah, Hilkiah had news for him. "I have found the Book of the Law in the house of the LORD." Hilkiah gave him the book to read.

Moses wrote five books. They are now the first five books in the Bible. These books were the laws of God.

When Shaphan returned, he had a surprise for me. "Hilkiah the priest has given me a book," he said. It was the Book of the Law that Moses had written! Shaphan read it to me.

I tore my clothes when I heard what was written in the book. We were not doing what God had commanded. I knew that God was very angry with us.

King Josiah tore his clothes because he was so sad and upset. They had disobeyed God and nothing could be worse than that.

"Go, ask the LORD for me about the words of this book which has been found," I said, "for the LORD is very angry, because our fathers have not obeyed the words of this book."

So Shaphan, Hilkiah the priest, and three other men went to talk to Huldah the prophetess. Huldah gave them God's answer.

A prophetess is a female prophet. She received and spoke messages from God.

"Thus says the LORD: 'I will bring disaster on this place and on all the people who live there because they have forsaken Me.'"

But God gave Huldah a special message for me from God. "Because your heart was tender, and you humbled yourself before the LORD when you heard what I spoke against this place, you [will go] to your grave in peace; and your eyes shall not see all the disaster which I will bring on this place."

I gathered all the people of Jerusalem together and we went to the temple. There I read to everyone the Book of the Law. Then I promised the LORD that I would obey the words of the Law and would follow God with all my heart and all my soul.

Everyone else promised to obey God, too. Our parents and grandparents had not obeyed God. But now it was up to us.

Think About This

When you know the right thing to do, but do not do it, that is sin. Josiah did not know he had been disobeying God because his parents did not teach him God's way. But as soon as Josiah knew what God wanted, he began obeying. We should obey God, too.

1 CHRONICLES

The Kingdom of David

Hi! I am Ezra. I was a priest. I led some of the people of Israel back home. We came from a long way away.

This book was written for the people who came back home to Jerusalem with me to begin a new life. First Chronicles tells about King David. Everyone needed to remember that David loved God and always tried to please Him. We were going home to rebuild the temple so we could worship God again.

I also wrote Ezra (named after me).

My Last Words of Advice

1 Chronicles 28

Do you think your mom and dad want you to be happy and to have a good life? Well, they do. That is what I wanted for my son, Solomon, too. I especially wanted him to follow the Lord.

I am King David. I had been king in Israel for a long time. Now it was time for Solomon to become king. I wanted my son to be as happy as I had been. But I knew it all depended on how well he obeyed God.

Would you like to know what I told my son before I died? I will tell you.

One day I met with all the leaders of Israel. I had something important to tell them. Of course my son, Solomon, was there as well. "Hear me, my brethren and my people," I said, "I had it in my heart to build a house of rest for the ark of the covenant of the LORD. But God said to me, 'You shall not build a house for My name. It is your son Solomon who shall build My house, for I have chosen him to be My son, and I will be his Father. I will establish his kingdom forever, if he [always obeys] My commandments.'"

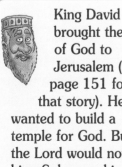
King David brought the ark of God to Jerusalem (see page 151 for that story). He wanted to build a temple for God. But the Lord would not let him. Solomon, his son, would do that.

Then I looked over at Solomon. "As for you, my son Solomon, know the God of your father, and serve Him with a loyal heart; for the LORD looks at all hearts and understands all your thoughts. If you seek Him, you will find Him; but if you leave Him, He will cast you off forever. The LORD has chosen you to build a house for the sanctuary; be strong, and do it."

 Solomon listened to his father's advice. For a long time he followed God. But then he disobeyed God. Solomon was punished for disobeying God.

Then I gave Solomon all the plans God made for the house of the LORD. Every detail was written down. I gave Solomon everything he would need to build a beautiful house for God.

"All this," I told Solomon, "the LORD made me understand in writing, by His hand upon me, all the works of these plans. Be strong and of good courage, and do it; for the LORD God—my God—will be with you. He will not leave you nor forsake you."

My son Solomon built a beautiful temple for God. And for a long time, Solomon obeyed God, too.

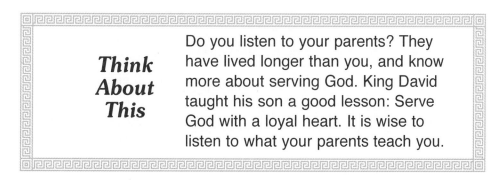

Think About This

Do you listen to your parents? They have lived longer than you, and know more about serving God. King David taught his son a good lesson: Serve God with a loyal heart. It is wise to listen to what your parents teach you.

2 CHRONICLES

God's Record of the Kings

I am Ezra. I led a large group of people back home to Jerusalem. We wanted to rebuild the temple. We wanted to worship God.

The book of 2 Chronicles tells about the temple. The people going back to Jerusalem needed to know about it. It tells about the kings who obeyed God and the kings who did not obey God. When we do what God wants, He takes care of us.

I also wrote the book of Ezra.

I Built God's Temple

2 Chronicles 2—3

I am King Solomon. I loved God very much, and I wanted to make Him happy. King David, my father, wanted to build a temple for God, but God would not let him. God told my father, "It is your son Solomon who shall build My house."

I would like to tell you about the temple. It was beautiful.

God had already given my father the plans to build God's temple. It was going to be a great temple because God was a great God.

I chose 150,000 men to work, cutting stone and hauling supplies, and over 3,600 men to lead them.

I also sent a message to Hiram, king of Tyre. King Hiram had helped my dad build his own house many years ago. "I am building a temple in the name of the LORD my God," I said. "And the temple which I build will be great, for our God is greater than all gods. Therefore send me at once a man who has skill to engrave gold and silver with the skillful men whom David my father provided. Also send me logs from Lebanon."

They were going to build the house with stone and wood. Lebanon had beautiful cedar and cypress trees. They were also going to cover the wood with silver and gold. The people of Tyre could help them with that.

I soon got a letter back from King Hiram. "I have sent a skillful man, Huram my master craftsman, skilled to accomplish any plan which may be given to him, with the skillful men of my lord David your father. And we will cut wood from Lebanon, as much as you need."

We began to build. The temple would be beautiful. It would be about 100 feet long, 30 feet wide, and 45 feet high. Everything would be covered with gold.

The temple's length was 1/3 the size of a football field. It was 5 stories high.

We worked seven years on God's house. For many years
we worshiped God there. God was great. Now His house was
great, too.

220

EZRA

Returning Home

I am Ezra. This book is my story. It is the story of God bringing us (the people of Israel) home to Jerusalem. Zerubbabel led the first group back. I led the next group.

I was happy to find the temple rebuilt when I got home. But I was sad that the people were not obeying God. We asked God to forgive us. We promised to follow Him.

The Parade Back Home

Ezra 1

I am King Cyrus. I was king of Persia a long time ago. Our country was the strongest nation in the world.

But I let some of the people return to their homeland. I would like to tell you why.

It was my first year as king. We had captured the land of Babylon. The people of Israel, God's people, were there. The temple they had built for God in Jerusalem had been destroyed—burned to the ground. I began thinking about this temple and the people of Israel. God was telling me to listen to Him. So I listened. God told me He wanted the temple to be rebuilt. I sent a message to everyone in Persia.

"Thus says Cyrus king of Persia!" I wrote, "All the kingdoms of the earth the LORD God of heaven has given me. And He has commanded me to build Him a house at Jerusalem. Who is there among you of all His people? Let him go up to Jerusalem and build the house of the LORD God. And whoever is left in any place, let the men of his place help him with silver and gold for the house of God which is in Jerusalem."

As king of the Persian Empire, Cyrus controlled all the nations on earth. But he knew God was really in control. He was king because God wanted him to be king. Cyrus knew that God wanted His people to return to their home. He wanted them to rebuild the temple. Cyrus was going to do what God told him.

Then I brought out all the things from the temple that the king of Babylon had taken. I gave them to God's people to take back to Israel—over 5,000 items made of silver and gold.

The king of Babylon had taken over Israel. When he did, he destroyed God's temple. But he took all the silver and gold out of it first. The silver and gold belonged in the temple of God. So Cyrus gave it to the people of Israel to take with them.

Their neighbors also gave them gifts. Over 42,000 people went back to Jerusalem to rebuild the temple. They took over 700 horses, over 200 mules, over 400 camels, and almost 7,000 donkeys.

Think About This

Sometimes people surprise us by obeying God when we do not expect them to. It is good to be reminded that anyone, even the king of a big powerful nation, may want to obey God.

NEHEMIAH

Rebuilding the Walls

I am Nehemiah. I was a special helper for the king of Persia. My job was to make sure there was nothing wrong with what he drank. The king was glad I was there to help him.

Later the king let me lead the third group of people back home to Jerusalem. We rebuilt the wall around our city.

Our enemies did not want us to rebuild the wall. They made it hard for us to do our work. I wrote this book so people would know how God helped us.

Rebuilding the City Walls

Nehemiah 1—4

I am Nehemiah. God gave me the important job of rebuilding the wall around the city of Jerusalem. Let me explain what happened.

A group of people had already rebuilt the temple. Now it was time to rebuild the wall.

The Persian Empire was very strong. The king of Persia controlled the whole world. He had been very good to the people. He even let some of the people of Israel return to Jerusalem to rebuild the temple.

The first group of people went back home to Jerusalem to rebuild the temple. To know how that happened, turn to page 222.

One day I asked one of my friends about Jerusalem, my hometown. He gave me bad news. The walls around the city were broken down, and the people there were very upset. That news made me so sad I just sat down and cried. I stayed sad for a long time.

Let me tell you about myself. I had an important job in Persia. I was cupbearer to King Artaxerxes.

I was usually happy when I was with the king, but the news about Jerusalem made me so sad that the king noticed something was wrong.

"Why is your face sad?" the king asked me. I was afraid to answer him. What should I say?

The cupbearer served drinks to the king. He was also responsible for the king's life. Before serving a drink to the king, the cupbearer would first taste it. That was to make sure there was no poison in the cup.

I opened my mouth and began to explain. "Why should my face not be sad, when the city, the place of my fathers' tombs, [is destroyed], and its gates are burned with fire?"

"What do you want?" the king asked me.

Before I answered the king, I prayed to God right there in front of the king. Then I said, "I ask that you send me to the city of my fathers' tombs, that I may rebuild it." The king let me go. He even sent letters asking others to help me.

Many people did not like our rebuilding the walls. People made fun of us, too. But that did not stop us. Then they attacked us. They tried to hurt us. Some of our group even had to stand guard while the rest of us worked on the walls.

"Do not be afraid of them," I said to my helpers. "Remember the LORD, great and awesome."

God did take care of us. We rebuilt the wall.

Think About This

Doing God's work can be unpopular or even dangerous. Nehemiah and his workers knew it was important to finish the job God gave them to do. They trusted God to protect them.

ESTHER

The Protection of God

I am Esther. I was queen in Persia when my family, the people of Israel, lived there. While I was queen, I was able to help save my family. God took care of us and kept us safe.

The book of Esther is my story. I am glad that someone wrote my story for the Bible. It explains how I became queen and how God helped me save my family. We trusted in God and God kept us safe.

Queen Esther Takes God's Side

Esther 2—7

Who is the prettiest person you know? The prettiest person in our country was my cousin, Esther. And being pretty helped her save a lot of our lives.

Let me explain. My name is Mordecai. I was helping to take care of Esther.

Esther and I lived in Persia. One day the king, King Ahasuerus, announced he was looking for a new queen. His servants picked the prettiest women in the kingdom to show the king. Esther was one of them! After all these beautiful women met the king, he made his choice. He chose Esther! She became queen.

Persia was a big kingdom. Esther and Mordecai were Jews, and their home was Israel. But the Persian rulers had taken over Israel and taken many of the people away from their homes.

I wanted to know how Esther was doing. And I wanted to be sure Esther was all right. So I stayed as close as I could to the palace. One day the king promoted one of his helpers, Haman, and told everyone to bow down to him. But the only one we should worship is God. So I would not do it.

That made Haman very angry. He made a rule that he would kill all the Jewish people in the kingdom. I was very upset. I went into the middle of the city and cried and cried. Esther did not know what was wrong. She sent one of the king's messengers to ask me.

If you bow down to someone, you are worshiping that person. You are treating that person as if he or she were God. God was the only One Mordecai wanted to worship.

I sent a message to Esther explaining the problem, and I asked her to talk to the king about it.

Esther sent a message back to me: "All the people know that any man or woman who goes into the inner court to the king, who has not been called, he has but one law: put all to death."

I told the messenger to tell Esther: "Do not think that you will escape death in the king's palace any more than all the other Jews. Who knows whether you have come to the kingdom for such a time as this?"

Soon Esther sent a message back. "I will go to the king, which is against the law. If I die, I die." So Esther invited the king and Haman to two special dinners.

At the second dinner, the king asked her, "What is it you want, Queen Esther? It shall be granted you. What is your request, up to half the kingdom? It shall be done!"

My cousin answered: "Let my life be saved, and the lives of my people. For we have been sold, my people and I, to be destroyed, to be killed."

"Who is he and where is he, who would dare to do such a thing?" the king asked.

"The enemy is this wicked Haman!" Esther told him. King Ahasuerus became so furious he walked out of the room.

Haman was scared. He knew he was in trouble.

King Ahasuerus punished Haman. I was given Haman's money and a special job in the palace. None of the Jewish people were killed.

Think About This

Doing God's work may mean taking a chance. Esther risked her position as queen. In fact, she risked her life to protect her people. God rewarded her by saving her people!

POETRY

Hi! We are David and Solomon, father and son. We were kings in Israel. We and other leaders in our nation wrote the Books of Poetry. Some people call them Wisdom Literature. We wanted people to know how to live. We also wanted people to praise God.

In addition to the books we wrote, someone else wrote a book about Job. Job was a special man who followed God.

JOB

Why Good People Suffer

I am Job. I loved God very much and always tried to please Him. God was good to me. He gave me a large family, a beautiful home, and many nice things. Then my problems began.

I lost everything I had, even my family. My friends told me that God was punishing me. But I knew better.

When you have trouble, remember my story . . . and trust the Lord.

I'm Glad I Didn't Give Up on God

Job 1—2

My name is Job. Have you ever had a bad day? I sure did. In fact, I had several bad days in a row. I would like to tell you what happened.

I loved God very much and tried to do what He wanted. I had a good life—a nice home, a big family, and a lot of nice things. I had it all.

Then one day everything changed. A messenger came to see me.

"The oxen were plowing and donkeys feeding beside them," the man said. "The Sabeans raided them and took them away—indeed they have killed the servants with the edge of the sword; and I alone have escaped to tell you!"

He was still talking when another messenger came up to me. "The fire of God fell from heaven," the second man said, "and burned up the sheep and the servants, and consumed them; and I alone have escaped to tell you!"

 Losing all his animals might not seem like a tragedy. But Job's wealth was in animals. When someone stole or killed his animals it was as if he were stealing Job's money.

Before he finished talking another man came to see me. "The Chaldeans formed three bands, raided the camels and took them away, yes, and killed the servants with the edge of the sword; and I alone have escaped to tell you!"

While he was still talking, another messenger came to see me. "Your sons and daughters were eating in their oldest brother's house," the man said, "and suddenly a great wind came from across the wilderness and struck the four corners of the house, and it fell on the young people, and they are dead; and I alone have escaped to tell you!"

I was so upset I tore my clothes and shaved my head. Then I fell to the ground and worshiped God. "The LORD gave and the LORD has taken away," I said. "Blessed be the name of the LORD."

That was the way of showing grief. When they tore their clothes and shaved their heads, that showed everyone how upset they were.

I still loved God very much. But soon I became very sick. I still never stopped trusting in Him. One day my wife said to me, "Curse God and die!"

"You speak as one of the foolish women speaks," I said. "Shall we indeed accept good from God, and shall we not accept trouble?"

I even had friends who came to see me and tried to tell me what to do. But I told them I would never stop trusting God.

Then God spoke to me. He reminded me of His wisdom in creating the world. He spoke of His goodness and complete power over evil. I was encouraged by God's words so I praised Him and kept trusting Him.

God blessed me because I trusted Him when life was tough. He gave me lots of new sheep, camels, oxen, and donkeys. He gave me more children, too. God took care of me just as He said He would do.

Think About This

When good things happen to you, do you thank God? When bad things happen, do you blame God? Job could have blamed God for all the bad things that happened to him. But he didn't. He loved God and knew that God loved him, too. We should thank God for everything we have.

PSALMS

Praises to God

Hi! I am King David. You probably remember me as the boy who fought the mighty giant Goliath. I loved God very much. God even called me a man after His own heart.

This book of the Bible includes psalms written by other people as well. It is a book of songs to help us worship God.

I wrote some of the psalms to ask God to help me with hard things. I wrote other psalms to thank God for taking care of me. Some psalms praise God for who He is.

PROVERBS

The Book of Wisdom

Hi! I am King Solomon. I was King David's son. God gave me what I asked. He made me wise. People came to visit me from all over the world. And God helped me solve their problems.

Proverbs is my book of wisdom. I also included some proverbs from other wise men. God helped me write Ecclesiastes and the Song of Solomon as well.

ECCLESIASTES

Do You Know How to Be Happy?

Do you know how to be happy? I am Solomon, and I was the richest man in the world, but I still was not happy. I tried to find happiness in this world, but I did not find it. I found the answer in God. Happiness is found by obeying God. I wanted everyone to know that. That is why I wrote Ecclesiastes.

SONG OF SOLOMON

Love

I am King Solomon. I wrote this book as a love letter to my wife. I wanted her to know how much I loved her. And I wanted everyone else to know it.

But I also wanted to let people know that God loves us, too. God's love is like the love I had for my wife. His love is really special. God will always take care of us.

THE MAJOR PROPHETS

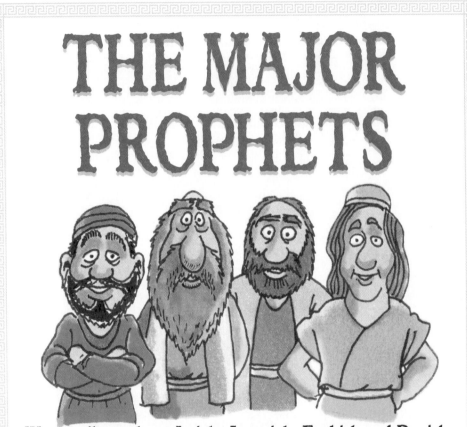

We are all prophets: Isaiah, Jeremiah, Ezekiel, and Daniel. We wrote five books in the Bible. We are known as the Major Prophets. Major does not mean we are the most important. It does not mean our messages from God are better than others. It means our books are longer than the books of the Minor Prophets. The Minor Prophets spoke most of their messages. Our messages were written.

ISAIAH

Salvation

I am Isaiah. I was God's prophet a long time ago. God gave me some sad and some happy messages for the people. God told me things to say about Jesus. I wrote: His name will be called Wonderful, Counselor, Mighty God, Everlasting Father, Prince of Peace. I also wrote that John the Baptist was the voice of one crying in the wilderness: "Prepare the way of the Lord."

My messages from God are in the book of Isaiah. I told how God was going to save the people of Israel.

JEREMIAH

The Weeping Prophet

I am Jeremiah. God chose me to be His prophet even before I was born. I had a sad life. I was threatened and put in prison. Then the king burned some of the things I wrote.

I had to tell the people that they were not obeying God and that He was going to destroy our city and our nation. But the people did not listen; they just tried to kill us.

The book of Jeremiah is my story.

They Told Me to Be Quiet

Jeremiah 36

I lived in the land of Judah during the hard times. I am Jeremiah. God wanted me to warn my friends that our country would soon be captured because we did not obey God.

They did not like hearing that. But I was just telling them the truth.

One day God spoke to me. "Take a scroll of a book and write on it all the words I have spoken to you."

I called my good friend Baruch. Baruch wrote what I told him on a scroll. He wrote everything that God had told me about what would happen to my friends in Judah.

When I finished, I said to Baruch, "Read from the scroll the words of the LORD in the hearing of the people in the LORD's house."

Baruch was a scribe. That means he wrote down the messages Jeremiah told him from God. Sometimes people were mad at him, too.

A scroll was a long piece of paper. Baruch could keep writing for a long time. When he was done writing, the scroll rolled together.

The house of the Lord was the temple. People went there to hear the words of the Lord. Of course, sometimes God's Word made them sad. Jeremiah was hoping these words would make them change.

So Baruch went to God's house. There were a lot of people there. Baruch read the words of God to them. Someone told the official leaders of Judah about the scroll. They asked Baruch to read it to them, too.

So Baruch went to see the officials. "Sit down," they said to him, "and read it in our hearing." Baruch read the scroll to them, too.

The leaders of Judah were scared. Baruch had told them about the king of Babylon coming to destroy Judah. "How did you write all these words?" they asked Baruch.

"Jeremiah spoke all these words to me, and I wrote them with ink in the book," he explained.

"We will surely tell the king of all these words," the officials told Baruch. "Go and hide, you and Jeremiah; and let no one know where you are." That is what Baruch and I did.

The officials told King Jehoiakim about our scroll. Then they brought the scroll and read it to the king. The king took a knife and cut the scroll. Then he threw the pieces in the fire. The king was not even scared.

The king sent some men to get us, but they could not find Baruch and me. God protected us and kept us hidden from them.

King Jehoiakim was an evil king who encouraged people to worship other gods. He did not obey God, and he died for his disobedience.

Then God spoke to me again. "Take yet another scroll," God told me, "and write on it all the words that were in the first scroll which Jehoiakim the king of Judah has burned. I will punish him, his family, and his servants for their sin."

So I took another scroll and gave it to Baruch. And again he wrote the words that God had given to me. It is a terrible thing to destroy God's Word. King Jehoiakim learned that the hard way.

Think About This

The enemies of God try to stop people from talking about Him. They destroy His Word. They think they have won and there will be no new Christians. But, God's Word can never be silenced.

LAMENTATIONS

Sadness for Our Nation

I was God's prophet during a sad time for our nation. I told everyone in Judah that God would destroy our nation. No one believed me. Our nation and our city were destroyed. God proved I had been right all along. But I was not happy. It was a sad day.

I am Jeremiah. The book of Lamentations is like my diary. Some people think it is the saddest book in the Bible. They may be right. It is very sad when people do not obey God.

EZEKIEL

Visions of a Happy Ending

My name is Ezekiel. I was taken to Babylon when my city was captured. I was still there when Jerusalem was destroyed.

God made me His prophet. I had many visions from God. Visions are like dreams. In my visions God told me what He was going to do. One vision was of dry bones coming to life. I told everyone what God showed me. Many visions were about Jerusalem being destroyed. Later I had visions of how God was going to bring our nation back together. He showed me the good times in the future. God never forgot us.

Dead Bones Come Alive

Ezekiel 37:1–14

I was God's prophet a long time ago in the Old Testament. God gave me, Ezekiel, special messages. I would like to tell you about one of them.

One day God brought me out to a valley. There were bones everywhere.

The Israelites were away from their home. They had been taken away from their home in Israel. In fact, their homes had been burned.

"Can these bones live?" God asked me.

"O LORD God, You know," I said.

"Speak to these bones," God told me. "Say to them: 'O dry bones, hear the word of the LORD! I will cause breath to enter into you and you will live!' "

So that is what I did. I spoke the word of God to those dry bones. Soon I heard a noise. Then there was a rattling! As I looked at the bones, they started moving and connecting to each other. Before my eyes, the bones were covered with skin. Then breath came into them, and the bones stood on their feet. Those dry bones became a huge army!

Then God said to me, "These bones are the whole house of Israel." God had not forgotten about me and my friends. He was reminding me that we would live again, and we would return to our homeland.

That was great news! We would not be away from home forever. We would be together again. God had not forgotten us!

Think About This

God knows everything that is happening to His people. Just in case Ezekiel thought God had forgotten the Israelites, He showed Ezekiel a vision. It was to remind Ezekiel that they were not alone. God was going to take care of them.

DANIEL

God's Plan for the Future

My name is Daniel. I spent the night in a lions' den. My good friends, Shadrach, Meshach, and Abednego, had some problems, too. They had to stay in a fiery furnace. But we all kept obeying God. He took good care of us.

I grew up in Babylon. My relatives, the people of Israel, were taken away from their homes by the king of Babylon. He wanted us to serve him. That is when I got into trouble. I wanted only to serve and obey God.

The book of Daniel is my story. People study my book because it also tells what will happen when Jesus comes back.

Shadrach, Meshach, and Abednego

Daniel 3

Do you like being different? Is it hard? My three friends, Shadrach, Meshach, Abednego, and I were different. Everyone was disobeying God. We did not want to disobey God. So we acted differently. We were far from our home, but God kept us safe.

My name is Daniel. I would like to tell you what happened.

One day King Nebuchadnezzar made a new rule. Everyone in the kingdom was to bow down and worship a new god. Shadrach, Meshach, and Abednego would not do that. They would only worship God.

Some of the people reported my friends to the king. "O king," they told him, "Shadrach, Meshach, and Abednego do not serve your gods or worship the gold image which you have set up."

 King Nebuchadnezzar was the king of Babylon. He also became the king over Daniel's homeland and brought them back to live in Babylon. He gave Shadrach, Meshach, Abednego, and Daniel important jobs with him.

The king's god was a make-believe god, called an idol. It was like a statue. It was made of gold and was almost 100 feet high! The king and other people worshiped it as if it were a real god!

The king was very angry. He demanded that my three friends be brought to see him. "Is it true that you do not serve my gods or worship the gold image which I have set up?" the king asked them. "If you do not worship, you shall be thrown immediately into a burning fiery furnace."

This furnace was different from an ordinary home furnace. This furnace was like a big box made of fire. Shadrach, Meshach, and Abednego were walking into the middle of a burning fire.

My friends said to the king, "If that is the case, our God is able to deliver us from the burning fiery furnace. But if not, let it be known to you that we do not serve your gods, nor will we worship the gold image which you have set up."

The
look on the
king's face
changed.
He was
really mad
now! The
king told
his servants
to turn up
the heat in
the furnace
so it was

seven times hotter than normal. Then they tied up Shadrach,
Meshach, and Abednego and threw them in the furnace.

The men who
threw my friends
into the furnace
were killed by the
incredibly hot
flames. But my
friends were not
killed.

The king was amazed. "Look! I see four men loose, walking in the midst of the fire." The fourth man was an angel God sent to protect my friends.

The king walked over to the furnace. "Shadrach, Meshach, and Abednego," he shouted, "come out and come here!"

My friends came out of the furnace. The king and all his friends gathered around them and looked. My friends' clothes were not burned. Not one hair on their heads had been burned! They did not even smell as if they had been in the fire.

"Blessed be the God of Shadrach, Meshach, and Abednego, who sent His angel and delivered His servants who trusted in Him," the king said.

God sent an angel to protect Shadrach, Meshach, and Abednego! Angels are God's helpers.

Think About This

It does not seem fair that people are punished when they have not done anything wrong. But that happens sometimes. God knew that Shadrach, Meshach, and Abednego had done no wrong. He protected them from the fiery furnace.

A Strange Place to Spend the Night

Daniel 6

My name is Daniel. I grew up in a country far from my home. Three times every day I opened my windows and faced Jerusalem, my hometown. Then I prayed to God.

One day I got in trouble for praying to God. I want to tell you how it happened.

One day some people came to see King Darius. They wanted him to make a new rule that no one could pray to anyone but the king. They knew that I prayed to God every day. They did this to get me in trouble with the king.

The men who wanted this rule were jealous of Daniel. They were looking for some way to get him in trouble. But Daniel was so honest that they could not find anything to criticize.

One day, after the king had agreed to the new rule, some people saw me praying to God. They went to see the king.

"Have you not signed a law that any man who prays to any god or man within thirty days, except you, O king, shall be thrown into the den of lions?"

"That is true," the king answered.

"Daniel does not honor you, O king. He prays three times a day."

The den of lions was a pit or hole in the ground. When the king's servants rolled the stone over the hole, there was no way to escape.

The king was very unhappy. He spent the rest of the day trying to figure out how to save me. But he had no choice. He had to follow his law.

The king was unhappy with himself. He knew the men had tricked him. He did not want to hurt me. But there was nothing he could do about it. The king was not upset because I was praying.

Soon the king's servants came to get me. They put me in the den with the lions.

"Your God, whom you serve all the time, He will deliver you," the king said to me. Then they put a stone over the opening so I could not escape.

The king did not eat or sleep that night. He did not even listen to his musicians. The king wanted for morning to come so he could find out how Daniel was.

Early the next morning I heard someone outside the lions' den. "Daniel, servant of the living God, has your God, whom you serve all the time, been able to deliver you from the lions?" It was the king!

"My God sent His angel and shut the lions' mouths, so that they have not hurt me," I told the king.

When Daniel was taken out of the lions' den, the men who tried to get him in trouble were thrown in it.

They took me out of the lions' den. The king was very happy now because he knew God had taken care of me. He wrote a new law: "I make a law that in every part of my kingdom men must tremble and fear before the God of Daniel."

Think About This

The men who were jealous of Daniel tried to get him killed. They had to trick the king because he liked Daniel. But God protected Daniel. Then everyone knew how powerful God is.

THE MINOR PROPHETS

We are all prophets: Hosea, Joel, Amos, Obadiah, Jonah, Micah, Nahum, Habakkuk, Zephaniah, Haggai, Zechariah, and Malachi. We wrote twelve books in the Old Testament. People call our books the Minor Prophets. This is because our books are shorter than the other books of prophecy. But we are just as important!

God sent us to tell our nation to obey Him. God was going to punish the people for disobeying Him. Many people did not like what we told them.

HOSEA

God Loves Us

I am Hosea. Amos and I were prophets to Israel. Israel was the Northern Kingdom. We tried to tell the people to obey God. But most of the people did not listen to us.

God used my marriage to Gomer as an example. Our marriage broke up several times. But each time God told me to take my wife back. It was just like God taking the people of Israel back. I tried to make people understand that. God loves us so much. He keeps taking us back.

The book of Hosea is my story. I wanted everyone to know what happened to me in my marriage. I am glad God helped someone write my story.

JOEL

Day of the LORD

I am Joel. I was a prophet of God in my country of Judah. Judah was the Southern Kingdom. Our country had lived through some hard times. But everyone still kept disobeying God. I told the people to change their ways and ask God to forgive them.

The book of Joel is my message from God. The apostle Peter used what I said to show everyone that the Day of Judgment was coming.

Peter referred to this time as the Day of the Lord when he preached after the Holy Spirit came on the Day of Pentecost.

AMOS

The Judgment Is Coming

I am Amos. I was God's prophet to my nation Israel. Being a prophet was not what I wanted to do with my life. I was a shepherd. But God gave me a message for the people of Israel. Things were going pretty well when I gave God's message to the people of my country. I did whatever I could to get this message across, but the people were so set in their ways they did not want to obey God anymore. They would have to learn the hard way.

The book of Amos is my message from God.

OBADIAH

Fighting Between Brothers

Hi! I am Obadiah. I was one of God's prophets in the Bible. I want to tell you about two brothers, Jacob and Esau. These two brothers were not at all alike. They never got along. Jacob's name was changed to Israel. His family became the nation of Israel. Esau's family became a nation, too. They were the nation of Edom. And guess what? The two nations never got along.

Israel became the children of God. The Lord blessed them. Then one day Israel was in trouble. Edom was glad that Israel had problems. So God gave me a message for Edom: Edom would be destroyed because they did not help God's people.

The book of Obadiah is God's message for Edom.

JONAH

God's Forgiveness

I am Jonah. God told me to give His message to the people of Nineveh. I should have obeyed God, but I did not want to go to Nineveh.

The book of Jonah is my story. I wanted everyone to learn from my experience. We should obey God the first time.

I Learned to Obey God

Jonah 1—4

Have you ever been told to do something you did not want to do? That was my problem. I am Jonah. I was God's prophet a long time ago in the Old Testament.

One day God said to me, "Go to Nineveh, that great city, and cry out against it." I did not want to go to Nineveh.

I decided to run away. I took a ship to Tarshish, not Nineveh. As soon as I got on the boat, I went to sleep.

Nineveh was the capital city of Assyria. The people in Nineveh were wicked. They did not love God.

God knew that I was not going to Nineveh. Soon the sailors noticed that the boat was starting to tip. The waves were bigger, too. And it started to get windy.

The sailors threw everything they could overboard so the boat would stay afloat. The captain found me sleeping. "What do you mean, sleeper?" he said to me. "Get up, call on your God to help us."

I went back on deck. Soon the sailors wanted to know if I had done something wrong.

I had to tell them the truth. "I am a Hebrew; and I fear the Lord, the God of heaven, who made the sea and the dry land." Then I told them my story and how I was running away from God.

"Why have you done this?" they yelled at me. I could tell they were really scared now. "What shall we do to you that the sea may be calm for us?"

I knew the answer. "Pick me up and throw me into the sea; then the sea will become calm for you."

 Before they threw Jonah overboard, the men prayed, "Please, God, don't let us die because of this man's sin."

The sailors did not want to do that. They tried rowing harder. But the harder they rowed, the worse the storm became.

The sailors finally picked me up and threw me over the edge of the boat. The storm stopped. Before I knew it, a huge fish had swallowed me!

I was in that fish for over three days! I had a lot of time to think and pray.

I thanked God for saving me. I told God I would obey Him. Finally, the fish spit me up onto the land. God spoke to me again. "Go to Nineveh, that great city, and preach to it the message that I tell you." I went!

I walked through the city. "Forty days and Nineveh will be overthrown!" I shouted. The people believed me. Even the king believed me. Everyone began to obey God.

God did not destroy the people in Nineveh. He forgave them because they obeyed Him. I was not happy.

God reminded me that He loves everyone. I learned that I should love people like that, too.

 Jonah actually prayed that God would let him die because he was unhappy about Nineveh being saved.

Think About This

Jonah found out that it is best to obey God, even if you do not like the job He has given you. It is not easy to obey when you are asked to do something you do not want to do.

MICAH

Judgment and Forgiveness

I am Micah. I spoke God's message to Judah. God said He was going to destroy it. The people were not obeying the Lord.

I also wrote about Jesus. You may hear some of my words at Christmas: "But you, Bethlehem Ephrathah, though you are little among the thousands of Judah, yet out of you shall come forth to Me the One to be ruler in Israel."

The book of Micah is my message from God.

NAHUM

Destruction for Nineveh

Hi! I am Nahum. I was God's prophet a long time ago. God gave me a message for the people of Nineveh. They would be punished for not obeying God. Nineveh was a big city in Assyria. The people did not listen. They were not afraid of anyone, not even God.

But the people in Judah listened. They knew that God is the strongest. They were happy to hear what I said. Assyria had destroyed Israel. So everyone was glad that Assyria would be punished.

The book of Nahum is God's message to Nineveh.

HABAKKUK

Questions for God

I am Habakkuk. I lived during sad times in our nation. Many of my friends disobeyed God. But God did not punish them. He was going to let Babylon destroy Jerusalem.

Now I had another question. The Babylonians were very bad people. Why would God let them win? But God told me they would be punished, too. I wanted everyone to know what God told me. So I wrote the book of Habakkuk. Many churches use my book when they worship God: "The Lord is in His holy temple. Let all the earth keep silence before Him."

ZEPHANIAH

Return to the Lord

Hi! I am Zephaniah. I was God's prophet when Josiah was king of Judah. He was only eight years old when he became king. He told our nation to obey God. Turn to page 197, and King Josiah will tell you how he did that. He and I were cousins. We worked together to help the people worship God.

Things were pretty bad before Josiah became king. So God gave me a message for Judah. The prophet Joel and I told Judah about the Day of the Lord when God will punish all who disobey Him.

The book of Zephaniah is my message from God.

HAGGAI

Rebuilding God's House

I am Haggai. I was God's prophet during a special time for our nation. We had lived in Babylon for a long time. But God had said we would return to Jerusalem. Finally, the new king let some of us go back home. King Solomon had built a beautiful temple. It was ruined when our city was destroyed. So a group of us went back home to rebuild it.

There were many problems. People were too busy with their own homes. But God said if they did His work, He would bless us. So we finished the temple. God told me the temple would be even more beautiful than the one King Solomon built.

The book of Haggai is my message from God.

ZECHARIAH

Building a House for the Messiah

Hi! I am Zechariah. I helped my friends rebuild the temple in Jerusalem.

God gave me special messages about the future, too. One night God showed me what was going to happen. He told me about the Messiah–Jesus. That is why the temple was so important. Jesus was going to worship God there!

God even told me about the Messiah's entrance into Jerusalem. When He came, people would cheer. He would be riding on a young donkey. Turn to page 356. Peter was there. He can tell you about it.

The book of Zechariah is the story of what God showed me.

MALACHI

Return to the Lord

I am Malachi. I was the last prophet of God in the Old Testament. It was over 400 years before another prophet spoke God's message. John the Baptist was the next prophet from God.

The people were making sacrifices to God. But God was not happy. They were not sacrificing the way God had said they should. They were not obeying God in other ways either.

My book reminds us that we should always give to God a portion of what we have, because all we have is from God.

The book of Malachi is the last book in the Old Testament.

NEW
TESTAMENT

THE GOSPELS:
THE STORY OF JESUS

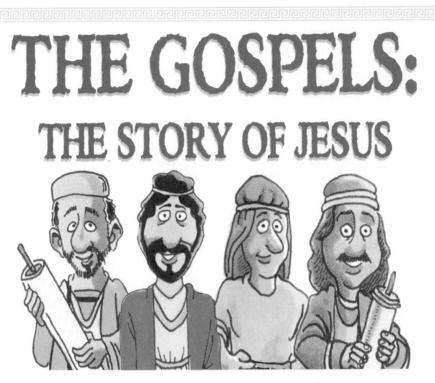

We are Matthew, Mark, Luke, and John. We are called the four evangelists because we wrote the four Gospels. The word *evangelist* means "writer" or "preacher," and the word *gospel* means "good news." We wrote our four books to tell the world the good news about Jesus.

Some of the stories we wrote about Jesus are the same, and some are different. The Gospels are the first four books in the New Testament.

MATTHEW

Jesus the Messiah

I am Matthew. I was one of Jesus' disciples. I wanted the Jewish people, the nation of Israel, to know about Jesus. So I wrote the gospel of Matthew. I explained how Jesus was related to King David in the Old Testament. I wrote more about the Old Testament than any of the other Gospel writers.

Jesus Is Born

Matthew 1:18—2:12
Luke 1:26—2:20

I am Mary.
God's Son,
Jesus, was born
to me. I will
never forget the
birth of Jesus.

One day an angel came to visit me. "Rejoice, the Lord is with you," the angel said. "Blessed are you among women."

His words worried me. I wondered what they meant. "Do not be afraid, Mary," the angel said. "You will bring forth a Son, and shall call His name JESUS. He will be great, and will be called the Son of the Highest."

The angel also told me that my cousin Elizabeth would have a baby, too. When I heard that amazing news, I hurried to Elizabeth's house. When Elizabeth heard my voice, her baby jumped for joy. "Blessed are you among women," Elizabeth said to me.

Elizabeth and her husband, Zacharias, were both old—too old to have children. But God made a miracle happen, and Elizabeth had a child. She named him John. (He was often called John the Baptist.)

The Roman emperor, Caesar Augustus, made a rule. He said all people had to return to their hometowns to be counted. This was for a worldwide census. Joseph, the man I was going to marry, and I were from Bethlehem. So we returned there even though my baby was due soon.

Caesar Augustus was the head of the Roman Empire. The entire world was controlled by him. When he said something, everyone did it!

Bethlehem is about an hour's drive from Nazareth. It took Joseph and Mary three days on foot.

Census is another word for count. Caesar Augustus wanted to know how many people were in his kingdom, so he had his officials record everyone's name and birthplace.

When we got to Bethlehem, it was full of people being counted for the census. All the rooms in the inn were taken and we had to sleep in the stable. That night our baby was born, and we laid Him in a manger.

The manger held the cattle's food. It was usually found in the stable, the place where people kept their animals.

Later that night some shepherds visited us. They told us an amazing story. While they were watching their sheep, a shining angel suddenly stood right in front of them. The shepherds were very afraid.

Then the angel said, "Do not be afraid, for behold, I bring you good tidings of great joy. There is born to you this day in the city of David a Savior, who is Christ the Lord."

Soon the angel was joined by many more angels. They all said, "Glory to God in the highest, and on earth peace."

I pondered these things in my heart.

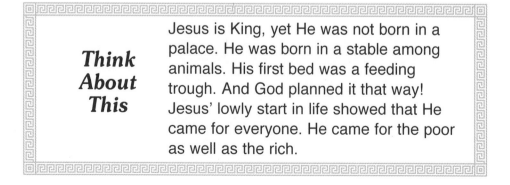

Think About This

Jesus is King, yet He was not born in a palace. He was born in a stable among animals. His first bed was a feeding trough. And God planned it that way! Jesus' lowly start in life showed that He came for everyone. He came for the poor as well as the rich.

Jesus Eats Dinner with Me

Matthew 9:9–13
Mark 2:14–17
Luke 5:27–32

I am Matthew. I was a disciple of Jesus a long time ago.

Before I met Jesus I collected taxes. Sometimes I made people pay more than they owed and I kept the extra money. Needless to say, I was not well–liked. Let me tell you how I met Jesus.

 People who collected taxes were not well–liked. They took more than the people really owed, and kept the extra money for themselves. They were not very honest.

One day I was sitting at my tax office when Jesus walked by. He looked me in the eye and said, "Follow Me." I stood up and followed Him.

One night I had a big dinner for Jesus at my house. There were a lot of other tax collectors there, too. We all sat down with Jesus and His disciples and enjoyed our food.

Because of their dishonesty, the only friends that tax collectors had were other tax collectors. But that did not bother Jesus. He wanted to be with them.

Our eating together made some people very angry. "Why does your Teacher eat with tax collectors and sinners?" the Jewish leaders asked Jesus' disciples.

When Jesus heard them talking, He explained the situation. "Those who are well have no need of a doctor, but those who are sick do," Jesus said to them. "For I did not come to call the righteous, but sinners, to repentance."

Think About This

Some people got angry that Jesus was eating with the tax collectors. But Jesus knew that sinners needed to hear about God's love even more than the people who already knew God.

Jesus Feeds 5,000

Matthew 14:13–21
Mark 6:30–44
Luke 9:10–17
John 6:1–14

I am Peter. Jesus taught me to love people. He loved everyone and always took care of them.

I would like to tell you about a time Jesus took care of a lot of people.

Jesus had just heard the news that John the Baptist had been killed. He took a boat and went to a place where He could be alone. It was not long before people found Jesus. After a while, a crowd gathered.

Jesus was not angry when He saw all these people. He felt sorry for them. Many people were sick and wanted Jesus to help them.

So Jesus began to heal those who were sick, and He taught all the people about God. Soon it became late. The other disciples and I realized that the people must be getting hungry, but we were in a deserted place!

John the Baptist had preached about the coming of the Messiah. He even baptized Jesus.

We explained our thoughts to Jesus: "This is a deserted place, and the hour is already late," we told Jesus. "Send the people away, that they may go into the villages and buy themselves food."

Jesus did not agree with our plan. "They do not need to go away. You give them something to eat," Jesus said. "How many loaves of bread do you have? Go and see."

We found some bread and fish. "There is a boy here who has five loaves and two fish," we told Jesus.

We gave the food to Jesus, and then Jesus told the people to sit down on the grass. He took the bread and the fish and prayed. Then He gave it to us and we gave it to the people. An amazing thing happened: we did not run out of food. There was enough for everyone. All the people ate until they were full.

Then we gathered up all the food. There were twelve baskets full of food left over!

Jesus fed over 5,000 people with 5 loaves of bread and 2 fish!

Think About This

Jesus showed by this example that it is important to meet all the needs of the people. We need to help with physical needs, such as hunger, as well as pass on the life-changing message of God's love.

Jesus Walks on the Water

Matthew 14:22–33

My name is Peter. I always tried to do the right thing. Many times Jesus had to teach me what to do. One time I was really scared, but Jesus kept me safe.

The other disciples and I were on a boat in the early hours of the morning. We had left Jesus alone on the mountain so He could pray. Suddenly we were in the middle of the sea. The wind was whipping us around, and the waves were crashing against us.

This was after Jesus fed over 5,000 people. Jesus told the disciples to go to the other side of the lake. It was the middle of the night when the storm blew up.

My friends and I looked out at the darkness. Then we saw someone walking on the water! We were scared. "It's a ghost!" we all yelled at once.

Then Jesus called to us, "It is I; do not be afraid." He kept walking toward our boat.

Could it really be Jesus? I wondered. "Lord, if it is You," I called back, "command me to come to You on the water."

"Come," Jesus answered.

I climbed out of the boat, and I began to walk toward Jesus. I was walking on water!

Then I noticed the wind. It was so strong that I got scared. I started to sink. More and more of my body was getting wet. "Lord, save me!" I screamed.

At once Jesus held out His hand and grabbed me.

"O you of little faith," Jesus said to me. "Why did you doubt?"

Soon Jesus and I were in the boat. As soon as we got in, the storm stopped. We all knew now who Jesus was. "Truly You are the Son of God!" we said.

Peter was fine as long as he kept his eyes on Jesus. He should have kept trusting Jesus.

Think About This
Peter had seen Jesus heal the sick and feed the hungry. He knew Jesus could do anything. He should have kept believing in His power. But Peter let fear make him stop trusting Jesus' call.

I Denied Knowing My Best Friend

Matthew 26:31–35, 69–75
Mark 14:66–72
Luke 22:54–62
John 18:15–18

I am Peter. Jesus was the best friend I ever had. I planned to be loyal to Him forever. But, something happened that scared me. Then I did something I will always be sorry for.

The Passover meal we had with Jesus turned out to be our last meal together before Jesus died. But we did not know that then.

That night after our dinner Jesus told us, "All of you will be made to stumble because of Me this night."

The Passover started with Moses. God wanted the people of Israel to remember how He saved them from slavery in Egypt. Moses would be glad to tell you more about this if you turn to page 56. This Passover was different. This was Jesus' Last Supper. And the first Communion.

"Even if all are made to stumble because of You," I spoke up, "I will never be made to stumble."

Jesus looked at me. "I say to you that this night, before the rooster crows, you will deny Me three times."

Peter was certain he would never deny knowing Jesus. But Jesus knew that before morning, Peter would deny Him three times.

I insisted that Jesus was wrong. I would never say I did not know and love Jesus! "Even if I have to die with You, I will not deny You," I explained. I was not the only one who felt this way. The other disciples said the same thing.

Later that night a huge crowd came to arrest Jesus. I ran away. So did the other disciples. Then I decided to follow Jesus at a distance. He was taken away to the temple. I stayed in the courtyard to watch.

As I was standing there, warming myself by the fire, a girl came over and looked at me. "You also were with Jesus," she said to me.

"I do not know what you are saying," I told her and walked away.

 The courtyard was the area right outside the building where Jesus was being tried. There were a lot of people there.

A little bit later another girl recognized me and said to the others around her, "This fellow also was with Jesus."

"I do not know the Man!" I said.

Later some more
people came over to me and said,
"Surely you also are one of them, because
your speech gives you away."

I started swearing, "I do not know the Man!"

Just then a rooster crowed. Jesus turned and looked at me. I remembered what He had said: "Before the rooster crows, you will deny Me three times." I went outside the temple courtyard and burst into tears. I had done what I promised Jesus I would never do.

The next time I talked to Jesus He had risen from the dead. What do you think He said to me? He told me to follow Him and tell others about Him. That is what I did for the rest of my life.

MARK

Jesus the Servant

Hi! I am John Mark. I am a cousin of Barnabas, who traveled with the apostle Paul.

The apostle Peter and I were very close. He called me his son. That was because he was the first one to tell me about Jesus.

My Gospel was written to the Romans, the people who were part of the Roman Empire. Much of what I wrote about Jesus I learned from Peter because he had spent so much time with Jesus.

Jesus Healed Me

Mark 2:1–12
Matthew 9:1–8
Luke 5:17–26

Have you ever wanted
something very, very
much? I did. I am a man
who was paralyzed, and
I wanted to walk. I knew
Jesus could help me.
And He did.

One morning I heard that Jesus was in town. I got on my bed and four men carried me to the house where Jesus was staying.

There was one problem. We could not get in to see Jesus because there were too many people in the house. So the men who were carrying me climbed up to the roof. Then they made a hole right above where Jesus was standing. As soon as they had made a hole big enough, my friends lowered me down in front of Jesus.

 The man's bed was probably a kind of mat. Because he was paralyzed, he had to lie on his bed all day long. People would carry him wherever he wanted to go. When he was not using it, his bed could be rolled up.

The roof was made up of tiles. To make a hole, all they had to do was move some of the tiles.

Jesus saw how much we believed in Him. He looked at me. "Son," He said, "your sins are forgiven you."

The Jewish leaders did not like that. Jesus knew that they were thinking, "Does He think He is God? Who can forgive sins but God alone?"

 The Jewish leaders refused to believe that Jesus was God's Son. They looked for things to criticize about Him.

"Why do you reason [wonder] about these things in your hearts?" Jesus said to them, "Which is easier, to say . . . 'Your sins are forgiven you,' or to say, 'Arise, take up your bed and walk'?"

No one said anything. Jesus kept talking. He told them He was doing this so that they would know He has the power to forgive sin. Jesus said to me, "I say to you, arise, take up your bed, and go to your house."

Instantly I could move my legs and arms. I stood up, picked up my bed, and walked out of the house.

Everyone was amazed. "We never saw anything like this!" they said.

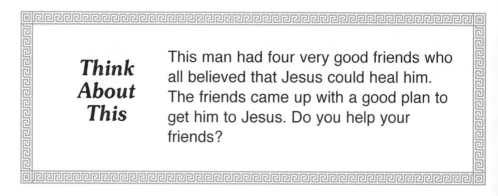

Think About This

This man had four very good friends who all believed that Jesus could heal him. The friends came up with a good plan to get him to Jesus. Do you help your friends?

Jesus Calms the Storm

Mark 4:35–41
Matthew 8:23–27
Luke 8:22–25

I am Peter. I was one of Jesus' disciples. I saw Jesus do many wonderful things. There were many times that Jesus reminded us in a special way that He was God's Son.

One time was in the middle of a big storm.

Jesus had just finished a long day teaching people about God. At the end of the day, we all got in a boat. "Let us cross over to the other side," Jesus told us. So we pushed off from the shore to cross the Sea of Galilee.

After a little while, a strong wind began blowing. The waves were getting high, too. The waves were so high that water was coming into the boat. We were starting to sink!

Jesus was asleep in the stern of the boat. Several of us woke Him. "Do you not care that we are dying?" we asked Him.

Jesus stood up. He looked out over the side of the boat. "Peace!" Jesus called, "Be still!" As soon as Jesus said those words, the wind stopped blowing and the waves became calm.

 The stern is the back of the boat. The disciples could not understand how Jesus could sleep with all the water filling up the boat.

They really should not have been surprised. Jesus made the wind and the waves. Of course they would obey Him!

"Why are you so fearful?" Jesus said to us, "How is it that you have no faith?"

Then we were even more afraid. We said to one another, "Who can this be, that even the wind and the sea obey Him?"

We continued
sailing until
we reached
the other side
of the sea.

Think About This

Are you scared when thunder is pounding
and lightning is flashing across the sky?
Jesus used the storm to show the disciples
that He had everything under control. They
saw that Jesus was God's Son.

Jesus Enters Jerusalem

Mark 11:1–11
Matthew 21:1–11
Luke 19:28–40

My name is Peter. I was one of Jesus' closest disciples. I had many good times with Jesus. One of my happiest memories is when Jesus entered Jerusalem riding on a colt.

It was the week before Passover. Many people were in Jerusalem for this exciting time. We were going there with Jesus.

Jesus stopped just before we got to Jerusalem. We were right near Bethphage. "Go into the village," Jesus told a couple of us. "As soon as you have entered it you will find a colt tied, on which no one has sat. Loose it and bring it. If anyone says to you, 'Why are you doing this?' say, 'The Lord has need of it.'"

A colt is a young donkey or horse. This colt was special. No one had ever ridden on it.

Passover was a special time in Jerusalem. Jerusalem was the capital city. At Passover, the people remembered how God brought them out of Egypt. Turn to page 56. Moses will explain more about it.

We went into the village. We saw the colt outside on the street and we untied it. Some people were standing there and saw us. "What are you doing, loosing the colt?" they asked us.

"The Lord has need of it," we told them. So they let us go.

We brought the colt to Jesus. Several of us put our clothes on the colt. Then Jesus sat on it, and we led the colt toward Jerusalem. As the people saw Jesus riding on the colt, they ran in front of us and spread their clothes (cloaks) in front of Jesus. Other people laid leafy branches on the road.

"Hosanna!" the crowd shouted. "Blessed is He who comes in the name of the LORD! . . . Hosanna in the highest!"

When we entered Jerusalem, the entire city was excited. Everyone in the city wanted to know who this Man was that was being so honored.

These clothes were mostly cloaks, or the coats they wore over their shoulders. There were no sleeves in them. It was easy to take them off and put them on the colt or lay them on the ground.

The word *Hosanna* means "Save now." The people were praising Jesus for coming to save them, but they did not really understand how He would do that. They did not know He had to die.

Zechariah the prophet had written about this event a long time ago. "Behold, your King is coming to you; lowly, and riding on a donkey, a colt, the foal of a donkey."

Zechariah was a prophet in the Old Testament. He told some of the things Jesus would do. He will tell you about it if you turn to page 305.

**Think
About
This**

One way to show that certain people are important is to roll out a carpet for them to walk on. Carpets are rolled out for brides and celebrities and members of royal families. The people treated Jesus like a king when they spread cloaks and branches before Him on the road to Jerusalem.

LUKE

Jesus the Perfect Man

I am Luke. I am a doctor. You may remember me. I traveled with the apostle Paul and learned a lot from him. He and I went around the world telling people about Jesus. That is why I wrote the Gospel of Luke. I wanted people to know the truth about Jesus.

The Gospel of Luke is a history book. It tells the details of Jesus' life. I also wrote the book of Acts.

Jesus Teaches the Teachers

Luke 2:39–52

Every father is proud of his son. But my son was perfect. He was God's Son. I was with Him during the early years when He was a child, but He belonged to God all along.

I am Joseph, Mary's husband. Jesus was born to us. He was very special. When Jesus was twelve years old, He did something that amazed us.

Once a year Mary and I traveled to Jerusalem with our friends and relatives for the Feast of the Passover. We stayed for several days and then returned home.

The year Jesus was twelve, we all went to Jerusalem for the feast. We traveled in a group. When the celebration was over, we began the long trip home. After a day of traveling, we did not see Jesus. We looked for Him among our friends and relatives. We still could not find Him.

The Feast of the Passover gets its name from the night the Jews were freed from slavery. To find out more, turn to page 56.

We returned to Jerusalem. We had to find Him! We searched and searched for three days. Finally we found Him. He was in the temple, talking to the temple leaders and teachers. He was asking them questions. The leaders and teachers were astonished.

We were relieved! "Son, why have You done this to us?" Mary asked Jesus, "Look, Your father and I have looked for You anxiously."

Then Jesus said something we did not understand. "Why is it that you looked for Me? Did you not know that I must be about My Father's business?"

The temple is like a church and the leaders are called rabbis. It takes many years of study to become a rabbi.

We finally returned to our home in Nazareth—all of us. We watched Jesus grow in wisdom and stature.

Think About This

The people in the temple were surprised that a young boy could know so much. Even Jesus' parents were surprised when they heard Him talking. Jesus taught His teachers!

I Baptized Jesus

Luke 3:1–22
Matthew 3:13–17
Mark 1:4–11
John 1:29–34

I am John the Baptist. Some people call me John. I had a special job: Getting people ready to meet Jesus. He was the important One. I wanted everyone to be ready for Him.

Let me tell you about the day Jesus came to see me.

I baptized people who asked God to forgive their sins. The prophet Isaiah talked about me a long time ago. "The voice of one crying in the wilderness: 'Prepare the way of the LORD.'"

Baptism is from the Greek word, *baptizo,* which means *dip.* People asked John to dip them in water to thank God for washing away their sins.

Isaiah and John the Baptist were prophets. A prophet is someone who tells what God will do for His people. You can read about Isaiah on page 257.

Some people thought I was the Christ, but I set them straight. "One mightier than I is coming, whose sandal strap I am not worthy to loose." I preached my message to everyone who would listen.

One day I saw Jesus walking toward me!

"Behold!" I shouted. "The Lamb of God who takes away the sin of the world!"

Jesus asked me to baptize Him but I tried to stop Him. "I need to be baptized by You," I said to Jesus, "and are You coming to me?"

Jesus explained to me that God wanted me to baptize Him. So I baptized the Son of God!

As soon as He came out of the water, the heavens opened and a dove rested on Jesus. Then God spoke: "You are My beloved Son; in You I am well pleased!"

Think About This

Do you have a nickname? People often get nicknamed because of something they said or did. John was called "the Baptist" because he baptized people. He baptized them to prepare the way for Jesus.

Jesus Is Tempted

Luke 4:1–13
Matthew 4:1–11
Mark 1:12–13

We all have been tempted at one time or other. Even Jesus was tempted. But Jesus did not give in to temptation. Would you like to know how?

Let me tell you what happened. I am Luke. After I wrote the story of Jesus, I wrote the book of Acts. It tells what happened when I went on missionary trips with Paul, another apostle like me.

Jesus was baptized by John the Baptist. Then God directed Him to go into the wilderness and stay for over a month (forty days). During that time He had nothing to eat, so He became very hungry.

The word *fast* means to go without food. People often fast when they want to spend time alone with God.

Satan appeared to Jesus. He knew just how hungry Jesus was.

He suggested a solution: "If You are the Son of God, command this stone to become bread."

Jesus did not follow Satan's advice. He told him the words of Moses: "Man shall not live by bread alone, but by every word of God."

Even though Jesus was the Son of God, He studied the Scripture. He was ready to answer Satan when He was tempted.

Satan made promises to Jesus he couldn't keep. Only God has the power to do the things Satan claims.

Next Satan took
Jesus up to a high
mountain and showed Him
all the kingdoms of the world.
"All this authority I will give You,
and their glory," Satan said. "If You
will worship before me, all will be Yours."

Jesus did not do as Satan wanted. He again quoted Moses:
"You shall worship the LORD your God, and Him only you shall
serve."

376

Then Satan tried again. He took Jesus to Jerusalem and set Him on the top of the temple. "If You are the Son of God," Satan said, "throw Yourself down from here. For it is written: 'He shall give His angels charge over You, to keep You.'"

Jesus still did not listen to Satan. He had another Scripture for Satan: "It has been said, 'You shall not tempt the LORD your God.'"

Then Satan stopped testing Jesus and left Him. Soon the angels came and took care of Him.

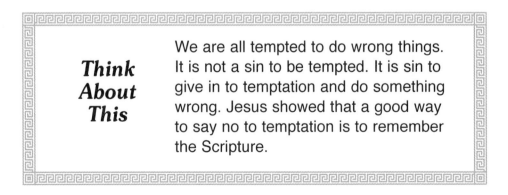

Think About This

We are all tempted to do wrong things. It is not a sin to be tempted. It is sin to give in to temptation and do something wrong. Jesus showed that a good way to say no to temptation is to remember the Scripture.

Jesus Heals Ten Lepers

Luke 17:11–19

It is no fun being sick. Nine friends of mine and I were sick and there was nothing anyone could do to help us. That is, until we met Jesus.

My friends and I had leprosy. Lepers had to live by themselves because everyone else was afraid of getting leprosy, too.

One day Jesus and His disciples entered our village. We all shouted at once as soon as we saw Him, "Jesus, Master, have mercy on us!"

 Leprosy is a skin disease. In Bible times, people with leprosy were thought to be unclean. Today the condition is called Hansen's disease, and doctors know how to treat it.

Jesus turned to look at us. Then He said, "Go, show yourselves to the priests." We all ran to the priests. As we were running, our leprosy was healed. God had healed us!

The priest was the only one who could decide lepers were well enough to return home and live among other people. Today a doctor would make that decision.

I stopped running. I had to thank Jesus. I ran back to Jesus and fell down at His feet and thanked Him.

Then He asked me a question: "Were there not ten cleansed? But where are the nine?" Not one of my friends had returned to thank Jesus.

Jesus looked at me and said, "Arise, go your way. Your faith has made you well."

Think About This

Jesus healed ten men of a disease that kept them from living close to other people. But only one returned to thank Jesus. If you had done something good for others, how would you feel if only one person said thank you?

Jesus Loves Children

Luke 18:15–17
Matthew 19:13–15
Mark 10:13–16

Every day I spent with Jesus I learned something new. Sometimes I thought I was doing the right thing. Then later I found out I was wrong.

I am Peter. I was a close friend of Jesus. I would like to tell you about a time I learned a lesson about children from Him.

One day Jesus was teaching people about God. As usual a crowd had gathered.

Jesus had become well-known. Wherever He went people came with their friends or family members. They wanted Jesus to heal them.

Parents started to bring their babies and other children to Jesus. They wanted Jesus to touch their children and pray for them.

The disciples tried to stop them. We told the parents not to bring their children to see Jesus. Jesus heard us. He was not happy.

"Let the little children come to Me, and do not forbid them," Jesus told us, "for of such is the kingdom of God."

Jesus said we need the faith that little children have.

Think About This

Sometimes important people only take time to talk with other people considered important. Jesus is the most important person who ever lived. He talked to children because He thought they were important, too.

I Saw Jesus

Luke 19:1–10

Jesus was very special to me. He loved me even when I had no friends. Jesus gave me a new life.

My name is Zacchaeus. I was very rich, but I earned much of my money dishonestly. I would like to tell you how I met Jesus.

I was the head of the tax collectors. I lived in Jericho. One day Jesus came to our city, and I wanted to see Him very much. I tried to see around the crowd of people, but I was not tall enough. So I ran ahead of the crowd. Then I saw a sycamore tree and climbed it. I knew Jesus would pass right by me. Nothing could stop me from seeing Him!

Many of the Jewish people did not like tax collectors because they worked with the Roman government. They also charged them more than was right and kept the extra money. To learn more about tax collectors, read Matthew's story on page 317.

Jericho was the city God helped Joshua defeat long ago. Rahab, who lived in the city, and Joshua can tell you more about it. Turn to their stories on pages 87-98.

A sycamore tree is a kind of fig tree. It has strong wide-spread branches. It is an easy tree to climb.

Then it happened. Jesus walked in front of me and stopped. He looked right at me and called, "Zacchaeus, make haste and come down, for today I must stay at your house."

I came down from the tree as fast as I could. My heart was full of joy. But people complained. "Jesus has gone to be a guest in the house of a man who is a sinner!"

"Look, Lord," I said, "I give half of my goods to the poor; and if I have taken anything from anyone, I will restore fourfold."

Jesus said to me, "Today salvation has come to this house, for I have come to seek and to save that which was lost."

Can a person who does bad things change into a person who does good things? Zacchaeus did. He stole money from people when he collected taxes. When he met Jesus, he wanted to pay back the stolen money.

JOHN

Jesus the Savior

My name is John. Jesus and I were very close. That is why I am called the disciple whom Jesus loved. Just before Jesus died on the cross, He asked me to take care of His mother.

Jesus called my brother James and me the sons of thunder. Thunder was not our dad's name, his name was Zebedee. Can you guess why Jesus gave us this nickname? We were not exactly quiet men.

I wanted the people to believe in Jesus and to trust Him as Savior. The book of John tells what Jesus said about being saved and about Jesus' death and resurrection.

Jesus Cleans the Temple

John 2:13–25
Matthew 21:12–13
Mark 11:15–17
Luke 19:45–46

I am Peter, one of Jesus' disciples. Jesus taught us to love God and also to love God's house.

One time Jesus showed us that God's house was to be respected.

During the Passover, we went with Jesus to Jerusalem. In the temple, people were selling oxen and sheep and doves. Other people were exchanging money. It looked more like a place of business!

The people used the animals to make sacrifices to God for their sins. We do not make animal sacrifices because Jesus is our sacrifice.

Jesus grabbed some ropes and made them into a whip. Then He started knocking over tables!

"Take these things away!" Jesus said. "Do not make My Father's house a house of merchandise!"

Jesus wanted the people to remember that God's house was not a place to make money. It was a place to worship God.

Think About This

What kinds of things make you angry? Jesus was angry because God's house was being used to exchange money and sell merchandise. Jesus said God's house is to be used for prayer.

Jesus Raises My Brother from the Dead

John 11:1–44

My name is Mary. My sister, Martha, and brother, Lazarus, lived in Bethany. I would like to tell you how Jesus brought my brother back to life.

One day Lazarus was very sick, so we sent a message to Jesus. It said, "Lord, he whom You love is sick."

When Jesus received our message, He was not worried. "This sickness is not unto death, but for the glory of God," Jesus told His disciples. He did not come to see about Lazarus right away. He stayed where He was for two more days.

When Jesus did come to Bethany, my brother had already been dead four days. My sister Martha went out to meet Jesus when we heard He was coming. I stayed inside the house.

Bethany is two miles away from Jerusalem. Jesus could have walked the distance in less than an hour.

"If You had been here, my brother would not have died," she told Jesus.

"Your brother will rise again," Jesus told Martha. "I am the resurrection and the life. He who believes in Me, though he may die, he shall live. And whoever lives and believes in Me shall never die. Do you believe this?"

"Yes, Lord," Martha said. "I believe that You are the Christ, the Son of God." Then Martha came to get me.

I came out of the house. When I saw Jesus, I ran and knelt at His feet. I began to cry. "Lord, if You had been here, my brother would not have died." All our friends who were with us cried, too.

"Where have you buried him?" Jesus asked us. "Come and see," we said.

Then Jesus
cried. Everyone
around us saw
how much Jesus
loved my brother.

When we came to my brother's tomb, Jesus commanded, "Take away the stone."

We hesitated. "Lord," Martha said, "by this time there is a bad smell, for he has been dead four days."

"Did I not say to you that if you would believe you would see the glory of God?" Jesus said to Martha. We moved the stone.

Tombs were usually caves or cut from rock. Lazarus's tomb was a cave. A rock was rolled in front of the entrance to keep animals out.

Then Jesus looked up to heaven. "Father, I thank You that You have heard Me," He said. After His prayer, He cried with a loud voice, "Lazarus, come forth!"

As we watched, my brother walked out of his tomb! He was covered with cloths from head to toe, and he could not even see.

 When a person died, the body was wrapped in strips of cloth. Spices such as rose oil and rose water were put between the strips. Finally, a linen napkin was laid over the face.

"Loose him, and let him go," Jesus said. As my brother breathed his breaths of life, many of those around us began to believe in Jesus.

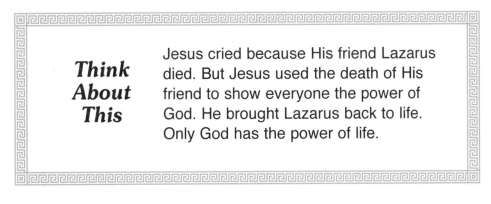

Think About This

Jesus cried because His friend Lazarus died. But Jesus used the death of His friend to show everyone the power of God. He brought Lazarus back to life. Only God has the power of life.

Jesus Is Crucified

John 19:17–42
Matthew 27:27–66
Mark 15:16–47
Luke 23:26–55

What was the saddest day of your life?

Let me tell you about the saddest day in my life. I am John. I was a close friend of Jesus.

All the disciples were with Jesus for the Passover meal. (Remember that we celebrated Passover every year to thank God for bringing us out of slavery in Egypt.) That night Jesus told us that He would soon be leaving us. We did not know what He meant. Later we understood that He was telling us He was going to die.

After our dinner, Jesus went to the garden to pray. Jesus was arrested and sentenced to die on a cross. God's Son was crucified like a criminal! I stood next to Jesus' mother. Jesus saw us standing together. "Woman!" Jesus called to His mother, "Behold your son."

The Roman Empire punished criminals by nailing or tying them to a wooden cross. Sometimes the victim's legs were broken to make death come more quickly. Jesus died before that could happen.

Then Jesus looked at me. "Behold your mother," Jesus said. From then on, Jesus' mother lived with me.

The sky became very dark even though it was the middle of the day. Darkness was everywhere! Then Jesus said, "It is finished!"

By dying on the cross, Jesus took upon Himself the punishment for the sins of all the people.

Suddenly the earth shook! And the veil in the temple tore in two. Then Jesus said, "Father, into Your hands I commit My spirit." Then He breathed His last breath. The Roman soldiers were scared. One of them said, "Truly this was the Son of God!"

The veil divided the temple. On one side were the people. On the other side was the high priest. The people were not allowed to go behind the veil. The high priest could go there only once a year.

Then Joseph of Arimathea, a follower of Jesus, took His body, wrapped Him in linen cloth, and put Him in his own new tomb (a cave). Then he rolled a large stone in front of the entrance.

Joseph was a member of the Jewish Council, but he believed in Jesus. Joseph cut a new tomb for Jesus out of the rock.

Think About This

Have you ever loved someone who died? Jesus' friends were very sad because they loved Him. Jesus understood their sadness. But, He had to die so we could live in heaven with Him someday.

Jesus Is Alive

John 20:1–18

I am Mary Magdalene. I loved Jesus very much, and He loved me, too.

I would like to tell you what happened after Jesus died on the cross.

On Sunday, I went to the tomb. It was very early in the morning. In fact, it was still dark. When I was near the tomb, I saw that someone had rolled away the stone in front of the tomb.

I ran! I found Peter and John, two of Jesus' closest disciples. "They have taken away the Lord out of the tomb," I said, "and we do not know where they have laid Him."

There were soldiers guarding Jesus' tomb. I thought they had stolen His body.

Peter and John ran to the tomb. I ran right after them. John got there first. He looked inside the tomb and saw the cloths that had been wrapped around Jesus.

When Peter got to the tomb, he went right inside. Then John followed him. There were the cloths that had been around Jesus' body in one place. The cloth that had been around Jesus' head was in another place. We did not know the Scripture that said Jesus would rise from the dead.

I was sad. I stayed outside the tomb and wept. Then I looked into the tomb.

I saw two angels sitting in the tomb! "Woman, why are you weeping?" they asked me.

"Because they have taken away my Lord," I said, "and I do not know where they have laid Him."

Then I turned around. I saw a man standing behind me. I thought he was the gardener.

"Woman, why are you weeping?" he asked me. "Whom are you seeking?"

"Sir, if you have carried Him away," I said, "tell me where you have laid Him, and I will take Him away."

The man looked at me. Then he said, "Mary."

It was Jesus! He was alive! "Teacher!" I said to Him.

He spoke again: "Go to My disciples and say to them, 'I am going to My Father and your Father, and to My God and your God.'"

I went and told the disciples that I had seen the Lord. Then I told them everything Jesus had told me.

Think About This

Easter means more than new clothes and family dinners. Easter is an important holiday. Every year in the spring, Christians everywhere remember and celebrate Jesus' rising from the dead.

Our Last Breakfast

John 21:1–23

I love to fish. In fact, for a long time I made my living by fishing. Then I met Jesus.

I am Peter. I would like to tell you about my last fishing trip.

One time after Jesus rose from the dead, I went fishing with some of Jesus' other disciples. We fished all night and did not catch a thing! Then the sun started to shine. We still had not caught anything.

Then a man on the shore yelled to us: "Children, have you any food?"

"No," we told him.

"Cast the net on the right side of the boat and you will find some," he called back.

The disciples fished with a net. They would put the net in the water, wait for the fish to swim into it, and then lift the net and the fish into the boat.

We took the man's advice and threw the net over the other side of the boat. As soon as we threw it in the water, the net was filled with fish—over 150 fish! There were so many fish we could not even get the net into the boat. John turned to me and said, "It is the Lord!"

John did not have to tell me twice. Soon I was out of the boat and swimming to the shore. Jesus had already started a fire and was cooking some bread and fish on it. I helped the others bring the fish to the shore.

"Come and eat breakfast," Jesus said.

After breakfast Jesus and I had a talk. "Peter, do you love Me more than these?"

"Yes, Lord," I said, "You know that I love You."

"Feed My lambs," Jesus said.

Jesus turned to me again. "Peter, do you love Me?" He asked me.

"Yes, Lord," I said, "You know that I love You."

"Tend My sheep," Jesus said.

Jesus was still not through. "Peter, do you love Me?" Jesus asked me.

It hurt that Jesus had to ask me three times. "Lord, You know all things," I said, "You know that I love You!"

"Feed My sheep," Jesus said again.

Jesus appeared to all of the disciples two other times. Read about the other times in John 20:19 and 20:26.

431

Three times I had denied knowing Jesus. Now three times I had told Him I loved Him. I spent the rest of my life telling people about Jesus.

 Three times Peter told Jesus he loved Him. Earlier, Peter had denied knowing Jesus the same number of times! Read about it on page 339.

Think About This

When you are given instructions, do you obey without questioning? Peter did—and he didn't know the man who was giving the instructions. He was very glad he obeyed when he caught so many fish. You will be glad when you obey Jesus, too.

HISTORY

My name is Luke. I wrote the history book in the New Testament. It is the book of Acts. It tells about the history of the church. I started by telling how Jesus said good-bye to His disciples. Then I explained how the Christians told everyone about Jesus and how the apostle Paul went around the world starting churches.

ACTS

The Beginning of the Church

I am Luke. The book of Acts is part two of my story. Part one is the book of Luke, which tells the story of Jesus. After Jesus left, we apostles went everywhere telling people about Him. God helped us.

I traveled with the apostle Paul on many of his missionary trips. When you read the book of Acts, look for the word *we*. Then you will know that I am with Paul. When I use the word *they*, I am talking about his work with other people. I was with Paul much of the time. So Acts reads like my own diary.

My book is sometimes called the Acts of the Apostles because it tells how the apostles told people about Jesus.

Jesus Says Good-Bye

Acts 1:1–11

Have you ever had to say good-bye to someone you love? It is hard. I am Peter, and I had to say good-bye to Jesus.

It had been forty days since Jesus rose from the dead.
During that time Jesus told us many things about God and
explained to us what was going to happen. Then it came time
for Jesus to leave.

One day the other disciples and I were with Jesus in Jerusalem. Jesus told us to wait there for the Promise of the Father.

The word *ascend* means to rise up. Jesus' return to God is sometimes called the *Ascension* because He rose up to heaven.

Then Jesus was taken up into the sky. He was going back home to be with God. We watched Him rise higher and higher. Soon Jesus was covered by the clouds. Then He was gone!

"Men of Galilee!" a voice suddenly called. There they were—two angels, dressed in white.

"Why do you stand gazing up into heaven?" they asked us. "This same Jesus, who was taken up from you into heaven, will return to you in the same way that He left."

The wonderful promise to believers is that someday Jesus will come back and get us. We will rise up to heaven as He did.

 The next story, "I Tell People About Jesus," will explain what the Promise of the Father was.

I Tell People About Jesus

Acts 2:1–47

I am Peter, a disciple of Jesus. He always helped me understand things.

Before Jesus left the earth, He told us not to leave Jerusalem. We would receive special power from God. So we waited. Would you like to know what happened?

The other disciples and I were staying in the Upper Room in Jerusalem. Jesus' mother, Mary, and His brothers were with us as well. It was the Day of Pentecost. There were many people in Jerusalem from all over the world. They spoke many different languages. It was a busy time.

The Upper Room was where the apostles ate their last meal together with Jesus before He died. This meal became known as The Last Supper.

Many years before Jesus was born, a man named Joel said He was coming to earth. You can meet Joel by turning to page 288.

The Day of Pentecost is 50 days after the Passover. It celebrates the first harvest of spring.

All of a sudden the sound of a strong wind filled the whole house. But it wasn't a wind at all. It was the power of God. I saw flames of fire above the head of each person. Then God filled us with His Spirit.

The city was in an uproar. Not only had the people heard the mighty wind, but they could all understand us, even though we weren't from their countries.

I stood up in front of everyone. "Men of Israel, hear these words," I shouted. "This is what was spoken by the prophet Joel. Jesus of Nazareth, a Man proved by God to you by miracles, wonders, and signs which God did through Him, you have taken by lawless hands and put to death but God has raised Him up. Therefore, let all the house of Israel know God has made this Jesus, whom you crucified, both Lord and Christ."

Jesus had at least four brothers, sons of Mary and Joseph: James, Joseph, Judas, and Simon. He also had some sisters.

Everyone was upset. "What shall we do?" they asked us.

"Repent," I said, "and let everyone be baptized in the name of Jesus Christ for the forgiveness of sins and you shall receive the gift of the Holy Spirit."

Thousands of people asked God to forgive them! Over 3,000 people believed in Jesus that day.

Jesus had told us that God would help us tell everyone about Him. Jesus also said that He would never leave us. It was true! He was there helping me tell people about Him. No one could see Him, but He was there. His power, His Spirit, was now inside of me.

Think About This

Jesus promised never to leave Peter and His other followers. He will never leave us either. If you ask Him, Jesus will always be with you, too.

A Lame Man Is Healed

Acts 3:1–26

Hi! I am John. Peter and I were two of Jesus' closest disciples. We had been together for a long time. Peter and I were together when we learned that Jesus had risen from the dead.

Now that Jesus had gone to heaven, Peter and I worked together to tell many people about Him. I would like to tell you about one of the first times this happened.

It was shortly after Jesus had returned to heaven. Peter and I were going to the temple to pray. When we got near the temple, we saw a man lying on a mat. He had not been able to walk his entire life. Each day he sat by the gate to the temple. When people entered and left the temple, he asked them for money.

People who were paralyzed during New Testament times didn't have wheelchairs. They had to lie on mats, and their friends carried them wherever they needed to go

As we entered the gate, he asked us for money, too.

Peter and I stopped. "Look at us!" Peter said to the man.

The man looked right at us. He expected that we would give him something.

Peter held onto the man's right hand. "Silver and gold I do not have," Peter said, "but what I do have I give you: In the name of Jesus Christ of Nazareth, rise up and walk!"

 When Peter healed people, he always said, "In the name of Jesus Christ." He wanted everyone to know it was Jesus who healed people. Without Jesus' power, he was unable to help.

Then Peter pulled the man up with his hand. The man's legs became strong and he leaped in the air! For the first time in his life, this poor man could walk! He went with us to pray in the temple. He did not just walk into the temple, he praised God and jumped up and down as he walked.

Everyone was astounded. "Why do you marvel at this?" Peter said, "Or why look so intently at us, as though by our own power or godliness we had made this man walk? The God of our fathers glorified His Servant Jesus. But you denied the Holy One and killed the Prince of life, whom God raised from the dead, of which we are witnesses. And His name, through faith in His name, has made this man strong, whom you see and know. Repent therefore and be converted, that your sins may be blotted out."

Many people believed in Jesus that day.

Think About This

The lame man asked John and Peter for money. Imagine how surprised he was when they healed him instead of just giving him money. When we ask God for something, He sometimes gives us even more than we asked for.

I Finally See the Light

Acts 9:1–19

What would you like to be when you grow up? I wanted to be a great religious leader. But God had a different idea. I would like to tell you what happened. I am Paul.

I tried very hard to follow what I had been taught about God. I studied the Bible. I learned a lot about God from my teacher, Gamaliel, who was very wise and knew a lot about God. I worked in the temple and taught people about God. I became very important, too.

Then some people started saying that Jesus was the Son of God. I did not believe that. I thought the important thing was to obey the Law of Moses. I did not believe that Jesus was the Messiah. But more and more people began to believe in Jesus.

The Messiah would be the next King of the Jews. The Old Testament had told the Jews to be expecting Him.

The law was given to Moses by God. It was a set of rules for the people to live by.

Other religious leaders and I told these people to stop talking about Jesus. We even killed one man, Stephen, because he kept talking about Jesus.

 Synagogues were places where people went to worship God.

Some of us took a trip. We were going to go into all the synagogues to remove everyone who believed in Jesus. But something happened on that trip that changed my life forever.

Suddenly there was a bright light in the middle of the road. It came from the sky, but it was not the sun. It was brighter than that. It was so bright I could not see. I fell down in the middle of the road.

Then I heard a voice. "Saul! Saul!" the voice called to me. "Why are you hurting me?"

"Who are You, Lord?" I asked.

"I am Jesus," He answered, "whom you are hurting."

I started to shake in surprise. "What do You want me to do?" I asked.

"Arise and go into the city," Jesus told me, "and you will be told what you must do."

Saul's name was changed to Paul after he believed in Jesus.

458

There was one problem. I could not see a thing. The men I was with helped me into the city where I stayed with a believer in Jesus named Judas for three days. Then one day Ananias came to see me.

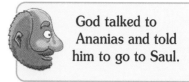

God talked to Ananias and told him to go to Saul.

"Saul," he told me, "the Lord Jesus has sent me that you may receive your sight and be filled with the Holy Spirit."

When I opened my eyes I could see. Soon I was telling people what I had learned. I told them that Jesus is God's Son, the Savior. I wanted everyone to know this great news!

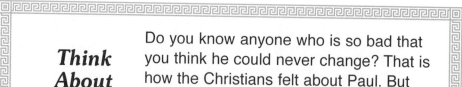

Think About This

Do you know anyone who is so bad that you think he could never change? That is how the Christians felt about Paul. But when Paul met Jesus, he did change. That is a good reminder that Jesus can change anyone.

The Angel Helps Me

Acts 12:1–19

Hi! I am Peter. I had a very interesting life. I spent many years with Jesus. He taught me a lot. Then Jesus went to heaven. "You shall be witnesses to Me," Jesus told us. Many people tried to keep us from talking about Jesus, but God took care of us.

I would like to tell you about one time God protected me.

The Jewish people loved God, but they did not believe that Jesus was God's Son. They did not understand that Jesus was the Messiah. So they were upset when we talked about Jesus. They wanted us to stop talking about Him. But John and I said, "We cannot but speak the things which we have seen and heard!" So we kept telling people about Jesus.

Messiah means *anointed one*. When the Jews anointed someone, oil was smeared on the forehead. That meant the person was set apart for God.

The Jews had not had a king for many years since being captured in war. They were looking for an anointed one to save them.

King Herod wanted to make the Jews happy so he put me into prison in Jerusalem. He was so worried about me that he told four squads of soldiers to watch me and make sure I did not escape! At the same time, though, other believers in Jesus were praying for me.

King Herod was the person in charge of the Jewish people. He was trying to make them happy by being mean to people who believed in Jesus.

One night I was sleeping in prison with a guard on each side of me. We were connected to each other with chains. Other guards were outside the prison door making sure I did not leave.

In the middle of the night I felt someone hit me. "Arise quickly!" a voice said to me. I opened my eyes and saw a bright light. Then I noticed an angel standing over me.

The word *angel* means *messenger*. Angels are God's messengers and helpers. They are powerful, but they are not as powerful as God.

464

The angel helped me to my feet. When I stood up, my chains fell off! "Tie on your sandals," the angel said to me. After I did that the angel said, "Put on your cloak and follow me." I thought I was dreaming.

I did what the angel told me. We passed the guards and went out of the prison. When we came to the gate that goes into the city, it opened by itself. We turned down one of the streets. Then the angel was gone.

I looked around. I realized I was not just dreaming. Here I was, out of prison, on the streets of Jerusalem in the middle of the night. "Now I know for certain that the Lord has sent His angel and has delivered me," I said.

I went to a friend's house. Many of the believers were together at her house praying for me.

I knocked on the door of the gate. Rhoda, one of the servants, came to answer it. When she heard my voice, she became so excited she ran inside to tell everyone and forgot to open the gate!

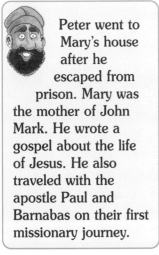 Peter went to Mary's house after he escaped from prison. Mary was the mother of John Mark. He wrote a gospel about the life of Jesus. He also traveled with the apostle Paul and Barnabas on their first missionary journey.

The other people at the house did not believe her. "You are beside yourself," they said to her. But Rhoda insisted that I was at the door.

I knocked again. This time some of the others came to open the gate, and they saw me. Everyone was shocked! I told them all how the angel had freed me from prison and how God had taken care of me. God had answered our prayers.

Think About This

Is there anything God can't do? He sent an angel to protect Peter. He made Peter's chains fall off. He opened the locked prison doors. God can do anything! What can He do in your life?

Giving My Cousin a Chance to Grow Up

Acts 12:25—13:13; 15:36–41

Do you ever disagree with your friends? I once had a bad argument with someone I traveled with for many years. Our disagreement was so bad we split up. Let me explain. I am Barnabas. The meaning of my name is "Son of Encouragement."

The Apostle Paul and I went on a trip together. We wanted to tell people about Jesus.

My cousin, John Mark, had spent a lot of time talking to Peter about Jesus. We took him with us on our trip, too.

We had some problems at our first stop, the island of Cyprus. A magician did not like our telling people about Jesus. He tried to keep the governor of the island from listening to us. Paul said to the magician, "Won't you stop talking against the truth of the Lord? And now the hand of the Lord is upon you and you shall be blind." Immediately the magician went blind.

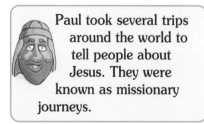

Paul took several trips around the world to tell people about Jesus. They were known as missionary journeys.

When the governor saw what had happened, he believed in the teaching of the Lord.

As soon as we got off the island, Mark left us and went home to Jerusalem. But Paul and I went on with our trip, telling people about Jesus. Then we came home. After we had been home for a while, Paul said to me, "Let us now go back and visit the people in every city where we have preached the word of the Lord, and see how they are doing."

I wanted to take John Mark with us, too. But Paul would have nothing to do with that idea because John Mark had left us during our first trip. No matter how hard I tried to convince Paul to take John Mark with us, he would not give in to me. We had a bad argument about it. In fact, we disagreed so strongly that we decided not to travel together anymore.

Paul decided
to take Silas with him
as his new partner, and
John Mark

John Mark
will tell you
about his
book and
more about
himself if you turn
to page 341.

and I went by ourselves. John Mark wrote
a book about Jesus. Later he even helped
Paul. At the end of Paul's life, he asked to
see John Mark because he was useful to
Paul. I believed in my cousin, John Mark,
just as Jesus believed in me.

Think About This

Has someone given you a second
chance? John Mark disappointed Paul the
first time they traveled together. But Paul
gave him a second chance. When we
disobey God, He gives us another
chance, too.

473

Saved by My Nephew

Acts 23:1–31

Hi! I am the apostle Paul. I loved Jesus very much so I wanted to tell everyone about Him. Many people did not want me to talk about Jesus.

I would like to tell you about one time I got in trouble for talking about Him. In fact, some men tried to kill me.

The Jewish leaders had me put in prison. One day they called me before the Jewish Council and ordered me to stop talking about Jesus. I made them very angry. I said, "I have lived in all good conscience before God until this day."

But they did not think that was true. They didn't believe Jesus had risen from the dead.

There were two groups of Jews there that day, Sadducees and Pharisees. I started a fight when I told them I was a Pharisee.

The Jewish Council was called the Sanhedrin. It was a group of more than 70 Jewish leaders who served like a court of law.

The Sadducees did not believe that anyone could be raised from the dead. The Pharisees believed people could be raised from the dead.

One of the Pharisees stood up and said, "We find no evil in this man." But the Sadducees did not agree. Soon the council members were arguing with each other and becoming angry. The soldiers who brought me into the meeting thought I might get hurt so they took me back to the prison for my own safety.

The next day over forty men met together. They went to talk to the council leaders. "We have bound ourselves under a great promise," they said, "that we will eat nothing until we have killed Paul."

They had a plan. "Now you, therefore," they said to the council leaders, "together with the council, suggest to the commander that Paul be brought down to you tomorrow, as though you were going to ask more questions about him; but we are ready to kill him before he gets here."

My nephew found out about the plan. He told me what the Jews were going to do.

I called to one of my guards, "Take this young man to the commander, for he has something to tell him."

My nephew went to talk to the commander. The commander said, "Tell no one that you have told me these things."

That night almost 500 soldiers were outside my prison. They led me to another city. After that I was able to go to Rome, the most important city in the world. I told people in every place about Jesus. God took care of me.

Think About This

Paul was not afraid to preach about God's love, even though doing so made other people angry. Paul knew he had to do what was right. So he kept preaching about God. We should believe in God and do what is right.

A Rocky Trip to Rome

Acts 27:1—28:16

Hi! I am the apostle Paul. I told many, many people about Jesus. The one place I really wanted to go was Rome, the capital of the Roman Empire. I wanted to tell people there about Jesus. Well, I did arrive in Rome, but I did not get there the way I wanted. Let me explain.

I was in prison for telling people about Jesus. Because I was a citizen of the Roman Empire, I was sent to Rome to be tried in court.

So Luke went with me. We got on a ship headed for Rome. There were 276 people in all on that ship. The weather was really bad. "Men," I said, "I believe that this voyage will end with disaster and much loss, not only of the cargo and ship, but also our lives."

The Roman Empire controlled the world. So Romans got certain privileges. One was that no one could send a Roman to prison without giving that person a trial first.

Luke was a doctor. He traveled with Paul a lot. Turn to pages 359 and 434, and Luke will tell you more about himself.

But the men would not listen to me because they wanted to keep going. The storm got worse. "You should have listened to me," I said. "Now I urge you to take heart, for there will be no loss of life among you, but only of the ship."

Later the ship was run into the ground. We all jumped overboard. The waves began to tear the ship apart. Some of us swam and some of us hung onto pieces of wood from the ship to stay afloat. Finally, we all made it to an island called Malta.

The people on the island were very nice to us. They built a fire so we could warm ourselves. When I put some sticks on the fire a snake bit me. I shook it off into the fire. The people on the island thought I would swell up and die, but I did not.

People listened to Paul talk about Jesus because He saved him from the shipwreck and the snakebite.

Later I visited a man on the island of Malta who was sick. I asked God to heal him, and He did. Soon everyone who was sick came to see me.

A few days later we left for Rome. I was able to tell people everywhere about Jesus. We trusted God to watch over us, and He did.

THE PAULINE EPISTLES

I am the apostle Paul. I once thought Jesus was telling people to disobey God. I tried to get rid of His followers. I was on my way to Damascus to arrest the Christians. All of a sudden, the whole road was lit up by a bright light. It was Jesus! He talked to me! I knew then that Jesus is God's Son. Now Jesus wanted me to tell people around the world about Him.

Churches were starting up in many cities. I could not stay with every new church, so I wrote letters teaching the people more about Jesus. My letters are called epistles. Some of them are called the *Pauline epistles.* The four books I wrote from prison are Ephesians, Philippians, Colossians, and Philemon—they are called the *prison epistles.* My letters to

Titus and Timothy are sometimes called the *pastoral epistles.* I also wrote Romans, 1 and 2 Corinthians, Galatians, and 1 and 2 Thessalonians.

On the next few pages I will tell you about the people I wrote to.

ROMANS

How to Be Right with God

I wanted to go to the city of Rome. Rome was the most important city in the world, but I had never been there. I wanted to spend time with the Christians there and visit the church. Since I could not go to Rome at the time, I did the next best thing. I wrote a letter, introducing myself to the church there. (I did go to Rome after I wrote this letter. In fact, I was in a Roman prison for a few years.)

The letter to the Romans is my first letter in the Bible, right after the book of Acts. It was not the first letter I wrote, though. I wrote it because I wanted the church in Rome to know what I believed.

1 CORINTHIANS

Problems ... Problems ... Problems

I traveled to many places telling people about Jesus. I spent a long time in the busy city of Corinth. The people in Corinth really needed to hear about Jesus. The first time I went to Corinth I stayed for one and a half years.

I helped start a church there. A few years later, some of the people from Corinth came to visit me. They told me about all the problems in their church and how the people were fighting with each other.

I wrote them a letter to help them settle their differences. First Corinthians is that letter. I answered their questions one by one, and I told them about love (in the love chapter, 1 Corinthians 13).

2 CORINTHIANS

Paul Defends Himself

Some people in Corinth did not like my first letter. They did not like my telling them to obey God. I was afraid they would tell people not to listen to me. So I wrote another letter, 2 Corinthians. In this letter I told them why they should listen to me. I wanted them to know I loved Jesus, and I wanted them to love Jesus, too.

GALATIANS

Jesus Is All You Need

On my first missionary trip I told people in Galatia about Jesus. Galatia was not very far from my home.

When I got home from that first trip I heard bad news. Some people were teaching the Galatian church things that were not true. They said believing in Jesus was not enough to get to heaven. I wrote to them right away. "I marvel that you are turning away so soon." I wrote, "Who has bewitched you that you should not obey the truth?" Then I explained why Jesus' death on the cross saves us from our sins and allows us to go to heaven.

EPHESIANS

Living for Jesus

I traveled around the world telling people about Jesus. I stayed in Ephesus for three years on my final missionary trip.

I thought of the people in Ephesus when I was in the Roman prison. I wanted to encourage them so I wrote them a letter. The letter I wrote is the book of Ephesians.

PHILIPPIANS

Joy

I visited Philippi several times during my missionary trips. My companion, Silas, and I were beaten and put in jail during our first visit. A big earthquake freed us.

The Philippian church people heard I was in prison.

So I wrote them a happy letter. I told them I loved them and God loved them, too. When you want to read about joy and happiness, read my letter to the Philippians.

COLOSSIANS

Jesus Is God's Son

I spent three years in Ephesus telling people about Jesus. About 100 miles away, a church was started in Colossae. When I was in prison in Rome, I heard about some problems there. Some people were trying to combine faith in Jesus with other beliefs.

So I wrote to the Colossians. I said that if they have Jesus, that is all they need.

1 THESSALONIANS

Believing in Jesus

One place I went during my second missionary trip was Thessalonica. My friend, Silas, and I stayed with Jason. Many people got angry. They started a riot, and the Christians helped Silas and me leave town.

Many people in Thessalonica had just started believing in Jesus. I sent Timothy to find out how they were doing. Timothy told me everyone was doing fine.

I wrote to them right away. I wanted to encourage them. I told them not to worry.

2 THESSALONIANS

Jesus Is Coming Again

In 1 Thessalonians I wrote how wonderful it will be when Jesus returns. But the people who read my letter thought Jesus was coming right away. Some of them thought that they had missed Him! Some members of the church even quit their jobs to wait for the Lord to come.

I had to write another letter. I told them the whole world will know when Jesus returns. No one is going to miss it. We should not be lazy while we wait.

1 TIMOTHY

A Pastor's Leadership Manual

Timothy and I were close friends. I called him my son. Timothy traveled with me for awhile until I left him at Ephesus.

I knew how hard it was to help people follow Jesus, and I wanted Timothy to be ready. So I wrote a letter to him. I told him to live a good life and be a good example. I told him not to let anyone look down on him because he was young.

2 TIMOTHY

Farewell

Second Timothy was the last letter I wrote. I was in prison in Rome, and I knew I would soon die. I wanted to be with Jesus, but I was sad to leave my friends, especially Timothy.

I wanted to prepare Timothy for the tough times ahead. I told Timothy to be strong. I told him to obey the Bible and to follow God. God would help him just like He had always helped me.

TITUS

Organizing the Church

I needed someone to help me teach new Christians.

Titus loved Jesus very much. He wanted to tell other people about Him, too, so he traveled with me. Later, I asked Titus to help the new Christians on the island of Crete. I told Titus to teach them how to live for Jesus.

The book of Titus is my letter of teaching to my young friend. I explained how to organize the church.

PHILEMON

Forgiveness

I told Philemon about Jesus, and he became a good friend. When I was in prison in Rome I met his slave, Onesimus, who had run away. I told Onesimus about Jesus, too. Onesimus was afraid he was in trouble because he ran away. So I wrote a letter to Philemon. I told him that his slave was now a Christian brother, and I asked him to forgive him.

My letter is called the book of Philemon. It is a personal letter.

THE GENERAL EPISTLES

Hi! We are James, Peter, John, and Jude. We wrote most of the general epistles. *Epistle* is a big word for "letter." People call our books the general epistles. Sometimes people call them the non-Pauline epistles. That is because Paul wrote the other letters in the New Testament. The letters we wrote are named after us. (We did not write the letter to the Hebrews. It was written by a Jewish Christian.)

We all spent time with Jesus when He lived on earth. But we did not understand everything He said. After Jesus rose from the dead, we understood things better.

HEBREWS

Jesus Is Better than Rules

We are Jewish Christians. Jesus was Jewish, too, but many Jewish people did not believe in Him. Some people told us that believing in Jesus was not enough. We had to follow the Jewish rules, too.

One day we received a letter from a Jewish Christian. The letter said Jesus is better than our Jewish rules; Jesus is our Savior. Rules do not save us; Jesus saves us.

That letter became the book of Hebrews.

JAMES

Faith that Works

I am James. I was Jesus' brother. I was in the Upper Room on the Day of Pentecost when Peter told the people about Jesus.

I wrote to the Jewish people who believed in Jesus. I reminded them they could not act any way they wanted.

In my letter I told them how to live good lives: They should watch what they say, and they should be careful how they treat people.

503

1 PETER

Suffering for Christians

I am the apostle Peter. I was one of Jesus' disciples. After Jesus died and was resurrected, the Holy Spirit helped me tell many people about Jesus. I spent the rest of my life telling people about Him.

It was not easy! Many people got angry when I talked about Jesus. I was even put in jail. I knew other Christians had problems too. I did not want them to give up so I wrote them a letter to encourage them. I told them that God allows suffering because it helps us be better Christians.

2 PETER

Holding On to the Truth

I was near the end of my life. I had told many people about Jesus. Then I heard that some people were telling Christians things that were not true.

Before I died, I wanted to set the record straight. So I wrote 2 Peter. I told the Christians not to listen to anyone who told them to disobey God. I reminded them that the Bible came from God. They should obey God.

1 JOHN

Christian Fellowship

I am the apostle John. I had a long life serving Jesus. I was called the disciple whom Jesus loved.

When we are close to God, we can become close to each other. That is why I wrote 1 John. (I also wrote 2 John and 3 John.) I knew the truth about Jesus. I saw Him die on the cross and I knew He rose from the dead.

I was about the age of a grandfather when I wrote my letter. I had known Jesus for a long time. The people I wrote to were new Christians so I called them my little children.

2 JOHN

Keeping the Faith

I was with Jesus during all that happened while He was on earth. Peter and I even had a race to Jesus' empty tomb after Jesus rose from the dead.

Some Christians were letting people stay in their homes who were teaching things that were not true. I wrote to them and told them not to listen to people who do not teach the truth.

My letter is called 2 John. Do you know people who are saying not to believe in Jesus? Then my advice is good for you, too!

3 JOHN

Being on God's Side

Many people loved Jesus, but some did not like what Peter and I taught.

I sent Christians out to tell people about Jesus just as Jesus had sent us out. I wrote a letter thanking the ones who had helped the Christians and scolding those who did not help.

My thank-you note, called 3 John, is in the Bible.

JUDE

Stand Up for Jesus

Hi! My name is Jude.

I was planning to write a letter about Jesus, my brother. I knew that He had died for my sins and yours. That was what I was planning to write about in my letter. But then I heard about some people who were telling lies about Jesus. I decided to write something different instead.

I reminded people that when people do not obey God they are punished. I wanted my readers to stay true to God.

PROPHECY

Have you ever wondered about the future? I did. I am John the apostle. I wrote five books in the New Testament, and I was one of Jesus' closest disciples. After Jesus died and was resurrected, His mother came to live with me.

Jesus showed me what would happen in the future, and I wrote it down in the book of Revelation. My book is the last book in the New Testament. Many people call my book the book of prophecy. (Prophecy is telling what will happen in the future.) There are seventeen books of prophecy in the Old Testament. But my book is the only one in the New Testament.

REVELATION

The End Is Coming

I loved Jesus very much, and I was looking forward to Jesus' return to earth.

One day I had a dream. Jesus showed me what was going to happen. Jesus would come, sinners would be punished, and Christians would be with Jesus. I wanted to tell everyone what I saw so I wrote the book of Revelation.

I ended my book with these words: Even so, come, Lord Jesus! That is not only the end of my book, but it is also the end of God's book, the Bible.

Index of People

The following people are mentioned in
My First Study Bible.

Index of Bible Events

My First Study Bible is filled with many exciting and inspiring events. These events are arranged according to the narrators.

Index of Animals

Even animals play a part in God's plans. The following animals are mentioned in *My First Study Bible.*

Index of Things

The following things are mentioned in
My First Study Bible.